Mastering DynamoDB

Master the intricacies of the NoSQL database DynamoDB to take advantage of its fast performance and seamless scalability

Tanmay Deshpande

PUBLISHING

BIRMINGHAM - MUMBAI

Mastering DynamoDB

First published: August 2014

Production reference: 1180814

Published by Packt Publishing Ltd.
Livery Place
35 Livery Street
Birmingham B3 2PB, UK.

ISBN 978-1-78355-195-8

www.packtpub.com

Cover image by Pratyush Mohanta (tysoncinematics@gmail.com)

Credits

Author
Tanmay Deshpande

Reviewers
Sathish Kumar Palanisamy
Mariusz Przydatek
Victor Quinn, J.D.

Commissioning Editor
Pramila Balan

Acquisition Editor
Subho Gupta

Content Development Editor
Adrian Raposo

Technical Editors
Veena Pagare
Shruti Rawool
Anand Singh

Copy Editors
Sarang Chari
Gladson Monteiro
Deepa Nambiar

Project Coordinator
Sanchita Mandal

Proofreaders
Ameesha Green
Sandra Hopper
Amy Johnson

Indexer
Mariammal Chettiyar

Graphics
Ronak Dhruv
Disha Haria
Abhinash Sahu

Production Coordinator
Manu Joseph

Cover Work
Manu Joseph

Foreword

The database technology world has evolved tremendously over the last decade. In the recent few years, there has been a huge data explosion that is driven primarily by data mining businesses and data generated by the proliferation of mobile and social applications. While the volumes have increased beyond anyone's imagination, the way we access the information of this data and the expected user experience has also changed phenomenally. For instance, when you search for information, you subconsciously use natural language text and expect to see what you were looking for on the first page, all within the blink of an eye. Also, you want this experience on a mobile device as well, even when not connected to your home and office network. So, modern applications can no longer use the traditional relational database to achieve the scale and speed that these applications demand. Welcome to the world of NoSQL!

While there are several open source NoSQL solutions available, such as Cassandra and MongoDB, in this book, Tanmay Deshpande introduces Amazon AWS DynamoDB, which is currently in development. DynamoDB is an excellent implementation of NoSQL available as a cloud service. This book should be a must have in a cloud programmer's toolkit, especially for those seeking to scale up their existing mobile cloud applications on the AWS cloud platform.

So what does a programmer expect out of a technical book? I'll draw an analogy using cookbooks. You see most cookbooks with beautiful and enticing recipe pictures; however, when you try the recipes, even if you are able to complete the book, the outcome will be totally different. The recipes are not customized to the reader's level of ability and local accessibility to the ingredients and kitchen appliances. There are technical and programming books too that suffer similarly. Not only should a programming book be easy to read and follow, the programmer should also be able to meet his real-life product development requirements.

I know the author well, and most importantly, he is a programmer by trade. This is his second book on the topic of Big Data. He has learned from readers' feedback from his previous book. I believe this book has all the coding samples that are tried and tested before they were included in the book. This book endeavors to guide the programmer through practical step-by-step processes that a software programmer would go through to speed up NoSQL integration.

I can't wait to try out DynamoDB myself, and I am sure you will find this book useful to transition from relational to NoSQL database.

Constancio Fernandes
Sr. Director Development, Data Center Security, Symantec

About the Author

Tanmay Deshpande is a Hadoop and Big Data evangelist. He currently works with Symantec Corporation as a software engineer in Pune, India. He has an interest in a wide range of technologies, such as Hadoop, Hive, Pig, NoSQL databases, Mahout, Sqoop, Java, cloud computing, and so on. He has vast experience in application development in various domains, such as finance, telecom, manufacturing, security, and retail. He enjoys solving machine-learning problems and spends his time reading anything that he can get his hands on. He has a great interest in open source technologies and has been promoting them through his talks. He has been invited to various computer science colleges to conduct brainstorming sessions with students on the latest technologies.

Before Symantec Corporation, he worked with Infosys, where he worked as the Lead Big Data / Cloud Developer and was a core team member of the Infosys Big Data Edge platform. Through his innovative thinking and dynamic leadership, he has successfully completed various projects.

Before he wrote this book, he also wrote *Cloud Computing*, which is a course-cum-textbook for computer graduate students in their final year at Pune University.

Acknowledgments

First and foremost, I would like to thank my wife Sneha for standing beside me through thick and thin. She has been the source of inspiration and motivation to achieve bigger and better in life. I appreciate her patience to allow me to dedicate more time towards the book and understanding what it means to me, without any complaints. I would like to dedicate this book to her.

I would like to thank my mom, Mrs. Manisha Deshpande, my dad, Mr. Avinash Deshpande, and my brother, Sakalya, for encouraging me to follow my ambitions and making me what I am today.

I would also like to thank my leaders, Shantanu Ghosh, Constancio Fernandes, Shubhabrata Mohanty, and Nitin Bajaj, for their encouragement and support. Also, I thank my coworkers for their support and motivation.

Above all, I would like thank the Almighty for giving me power to believe in my passion and pursue my dreams. This would not have been possible without the faith I have in you!

About the Reviewers

Sathish Kumar Palanisamy is an experienced, enthusiastic engineer and entrepreneur. Currently, he works at `Amazon.com` and solves complex machine-learning-related problems.

He thrives on coming up with fresh ideas. He developed many websites, apps, and gave them back to the community.

He is the founder of Flair Labs (an India-based start-up that thrives to achieve excellence in the field of engineering). You can find more information about him at `devSathish.com` or follow his tweets (`@devsathish`).

> I would like to thank all my colleagues and friends who helped me to gain knowledge in software engineering.

Mariusz Przydatek is an entrepreneur and technology enthusiast. For the last year and a half, he was designing and implementing the `Gamebrain.com` platform, a new cloud offering for the mobile gaming industry. Prior to that, he spent 7 years managing software development teams at Sabre Holdings, Inc. (SABR), a travel industry leader, owner of Travelocity and Lastminute.com brands.

Victor Quinn, J.D. is a technology leader, programmer, and systems architect, whose area of expertise is in leading teams to build APIs and backend systems.

Currently, he is building the API and backend system for SocialRadar, a group of start-up building mobile apps that provide real-time information on the people around you.

Prior to joining SocialRadar, Victor led a rewrite of the financial processing online forms and API for NGP VAN, a company that processed billions of dollars in campaign contributions during the 2012 election year. The system he orchestrated is on track to process even more contributions in the coming election years. He led his team to build this system, which included auto-filling and a sign-on system, enabling future contributions with a single click. All of these features were rolled up in a JavaScript single page app, embedding a fully functional payment-processing form into even a static web page with a single tag.

He has spent many years honing his skills with command-line tools, such as tmux in order to be maximally efficient in his work. His editor of choice is Emacs, and he uses the Dvorak keyboard layout.

He has Bachelor of Science degrees, one in Physics and the other in Computer Science from the University of Massachusetts, Amherst, and is a Juris Doctor with a focus on Intellectual Property Law from Western New England University. He is an eagle scout and a registered patent agent.

He lives in the Washington, D.C. metro area with his wife and Great Dane. There he enjoys brewing his own beer and riding his Harley.

Thank you to my amazing wife, Susan.

---

www.PacktPub.com

Support files, eBooks, discount offers, and more

You might want to visit www.PacktPub.com for support files and downloads related to your book.

Did you know that Packt offers eBook versions of every book published, with PDF and ePub files available? You can upgrade to the eBook version at www.PacktPub.com and as a print book customer, you are entitled to a discount on the eBook copy. Get in touch with us at service@packtpub.com for more details.

At www.PacktPub.com, you can also read a collection of free technical articles, sign up for a range of free newsletters and receive exclusive discounts and offers on Packt books and eBooks.

http://PacktLib.PacktPub.com

Do you need instant solutions to your IT questions? PacktLib is Packt's online digital book library. Here, you can access, read, and search across Packt's entire library of books.

Why subscribe?

- Fully searchable across every book published by Packt
- Copy and paste, print, and bookmark content
- On demand and accessible via web browser

Free access for Packt account holders

If you have an account with Packt at www.PacktPub.com, you can use this to access PacktLib today and view nine entirely free books. Simply use your login credentials for immediate access.

Table of Contents

Preface

AWS DynamoDB is an excellent example of a production-ready NoSQL database. It is hosted on Amazon public cloud, so within a few clicks, you can create your table and get started with it. Within 2 years of its release, DynamoDB has been able to attract many customers because of its features, such as high availability, reliability, and Internet scalability. With the popularity of mobile applications, everyone is dreaming of publishing his/her own mobile app, so for all such developers, DynamoDB is a great option because of its cost effectiveness and usability.

This book is a practical, example-oriented guide that starts with an introduction to DynamoDB, how it started, what it is, and its features. It then introduces you to DynamoDB's data model, demonstrating CRUD operations on the data model. Once you get a hold over the data model, it enables you to dive deep into the DynamoDB architecture to understand its flexibility, scalability, and reliability. This book also enlightens you on how to use DynamoDB as a backend database for mobile applications. It also has detailed explanations on DynamoDB's security in order to make your applications secure. It is concise, with clean topic descriptions, plenty of screenshots, and code samples to enhance clarity and to help you try and test things on your own.

What this book covers

Chapter 1, *Getting Started*, highlights why we need the cloud-hosted NoSQL database, introduces readers to various NoSQL databases, and then starts with what DynamoDB is all about, what its history is, and its features.

Chapter 2, *Data Models*, introduces readers to DynamoDB's rich data model, its data types, and various operations one can perform using AWS SDK for DynamoDB with various languages, such as Java, .NET, and PHP. This also provides good detail on modeling relationships in DynamoDB.

Chapter 3, *How DynamoDB Works*, gives an insight into the DynamoDB architecture and the various techniques it uses to maintain its highly distributed structure, the ring topology, replication synchronization, fault tolerance, and so on.

Chapter 4, *Best Practices*, details readers on how they can save their money by making time- and cost-efficient calls to DynamoDB. It also enables readers to deal with DynamoDB limitations. It talks about table best practices, item and indexes best practices, use of caching techniques, time series best practices, and so on.

Chapter 5, *Advanced Topics*, covers detailed understanding of CloudWatch monitoring, use of Identity and Access Management for DynamoDB operations, creating and applying security policies, and the use of the AWS Secure Token Service to generate temporary credentials. It also details error handling in DynamoDB and how to set auto retries and exponential back-offs on failures.

Chapter 6, *Integrating DynamoDB with Other AWS Components*, enlightens readers about the AWS ecosystem, how they can integrate other AWS components, such as Elastic Map Reduce (EMR), S3, RedShift, CloudSearch, and so on, in order to have everything that they want to do with their application in one place.

Chapter 7, *DynamoDB – Use Cases*, provides readers with examples on creating an end-to-end use case, what technology stack they use, how they leverage DynamoDB SDK APIs, and so on.

Chapter 8, *Useful Libraries and Tools*, introduces users to some very cool, ready-to-use libraries, such as Geo Library, Transaction Library, and libraries in various languages, such as Perl, Python, Ruby, Go, Erlang, and so on. It also gives insights into useful tools that enable users to test their code offline, tools that enable auto-scaling of production applications, and tools that provide utilities, such as backup/archiving of DynamoDB data.

Chapter 9, *Mobile Apps Development using DynamoDB*, gives users directions on how to use DynamoDB SDKs for iOS and Android and helps them to build Internet-scalable mobile applications easily. It also provides various options on building a secure user-management technique.

What you need for this book

This book requires you to have a basic understanding of Cloud, Amazon Web Services, and NoSQL databases. It has code snippets provided in various popular languages, such as Java, .NET, and PHP. So, basic understanding of one of these languages is good to have. The content is explained in simple English and has been explained using diagrams, screenshots, and suitable examples.

Who this book is for

This book is for web/mobile application developers, managers who are considering undertaking a project on DynamoDB, the NoSQL users who are sick of maintaining the distributed clusters, and security analysts who want to validate the security measures imposed by Amazon.

Conventions

In this book, you will find a number of styles of text that distinguish between different kinds of information. Here are some examples of these styles, and an explanation of their meaning.

Code words in text, database table names, folder names, filenames, file extensions, pathnames, dummy URLs, user input, and Twitter handles are shown as follows: "This configuration option allows us to set the maximum number of times `HttpClient` should retry sending the request to DynamoDB."

A block of code is set as follows:

```
    // Create a configuration object
final ClientConfiguration cfg = new ClientConfiguration();
// Set the maximum auto-reties to 3
cfg.setMaxErrorRetry(3);
    // Set configuration object in Client
client.setConfiguration(cfg);
```

When we wish to draw your attention to a particular part of a code block, the relevant lines or items are set in bold:

```
AmazonDynamoDBClient client = new AmazonDynamoDBClient();

// Set geo table in configuration
GeoDataManagerConfiguration geoDataManagerConfiguration = new
GeoDataManagerConfiguration(
        client, "geo-table");

// Create Geo data manager
GeoDataManager geoDataManager = new GeoDataManager(geoDataManagerConf
iguration);
```

Any command-line input or output is written as follows:

```
mvn clean install -Dgpg.skip=true
```

New terms and **important words** are shown in bold. Words that you see on the screen, in menus or dialog boxes for example, appear in the text like this: "You can click on **Continue** to move ahead."

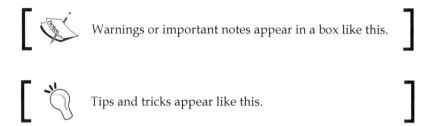

> Warnings or important notes appear in a box like this.

> Tips and tricks appear like this.

Reader feedback

Feedback from our readers is always welcome. Let us know what you think about this book—what you liked or may have disliked. Reader feedback is important for us to develop titles that you really get the most out of.

To send us general feedback, simply send an e-mail to feedback@packtpub.com, and mention the book title via the subject of your message.

If there is a topic that you have expertise in and you are interested in either writing or contributing to a book, see our author guide on www.packtpub.com/authors.

Customer support

Now that you are the proud owner of a Packt book, we have a number of things to help you to get the most from your purchase.

Downloading the example code

You can download the example code files for all Packt books you have purchased from your account at http://www.packtpub.com. If you purchased this book elsewhere, you can visit http://www.packtpub.com/support and register to have the files e-mailed directly to you.

Errata

Although we have taken every care to ensure the accuracy of our content, mistakes do happen. If you find a mistake in one of our books — maybe a mistake in the text or the code — we would be grateful if you would report this to us. By doing so, you can save other readers from frustration and help us improve subsequent versions of this book. If you find any errata, please report them by visiting http://www.packtpub.com/submit-errata, selecting your book, clicking on the **errata submission form** link, and entering the details of your errata. Once your errata are verified, your submission will be accepted and the errata will be uploaded on our website, or added to any list of existing errata, under the Errata section of that title. Any existing errata can be viewed by selecting your title from http://www.packtpub.com/support.

Piracy

Piracy of copyright material on the Internet is an ongoing problem across all media. At Packt, we take the protection of our copyright and licenses very seriously. If you come across any illegal copies of our works, in any form, on the Internet, please provide us with the location address or website name immediately so that we can pursue a remedy.

Please contact us at copyright@packtpub.com with a link to the suspected pirated material.

We appreciate your help in protecting our authors, and our ability to bring you valuable content.

Questions

You can contact us at questions@packtpub.com if you are having a problem with any aspect of the book, and we will do our best to address it.

1
Getting Started

Amazon DynamoDB is a fully managed, cloud-hosted, NoSQL database. It provides fast and predictable performance with the ability to scale seamlessly. It allows you to store and retrieve any amount of data, serving any level of network traffic without having any operational burden. DynamoDB gives numerous other advantages like consistent and predictable performance, flexible data modeling, and durability.

With just few clicks on the Amazon Web Services console, you are able create your own DynamoDB table and scale up or scale down provision throughput without taking down your application even for a millisecond. DynamoDB uses **Solid State Disks (SSD)** to store the data which confirms the durability of the work you are doing. It also automatically replicates the data across other AWS Availability Zones, which provides built-in high availability and reliability.

In this chapter, we are going to revise our concepts about the DynamoDB and will try to discover more about its features and implementation.

Before we start discussing details about DynamoDB, let's try to understand what NoSQL databases are and when to choose DynamoDB over Relational Database Management System (RDBMS). With the rise in data volume, variety, and velocity, RDBMSes were neither designed to cope up with the scale and flexibility challenges developers are facing to build the modern day applications, nor were they able to take advantage of cheap commodity hardware. Also, we need to provide a schema before we start adding data, and this restricted developers from making their application flexible. On the other hand, NoSQL databases are fast, provide flexible schema operations, and make effective use of cheap storage.

Considering all these things, NoSQL is becoming popular very quickly amongst the developer community. However, one has to be very cautious about when to go for NoSQL and when to stick to RDBMS. Sticking to relational databases makes sense when you know that the schema is more over static, strong consistency is must, and the data is not going to be that big in volume.

However, when you want to build an application that is Internet scalable, the schema is more likely to get evolved over time, the storage is going to be really big, and the operations involved are okay to be eventually consistent. Then, NoSQL is the way to go.

There are various types of NoSQL databases. The following is the list of NoSQL database types and popular examples:

- **Document Store**: MongoDB, CouchDB, MarkLogic
- **Column Store**: Hbase, Cassandra
- **Key Value Store**: DynamoDB, Azure, Redis
- **Graph Databases**: Neo4J, DEX

Most of these NoSQL solutions are open source except for a few like DynamoDB and Azure, which are available as a service over the Internet. DynamoDB being a key-value store indexes data only upon primary keys, and one has to go through the primary key to access certain attributes. Let's start learning more about DynamoDB by having a look at its history.

DynamoDB's history

Amazon's e-commerce platform had a huge set of decoupled services developed and managed individually, and each and every service had an API to be used and consumed by others. Earlier, each service had direct database access, which was a major bottleneck. In terms of scalability, Amazon's requirements were more than any third-party vendors could provide at that time.

DynamoDB was built to address Amazon's high availability, extreme scalability, and durability needs. Earlier, Amazon used to store its production data in relational databases and services had been provided for all required operations. However, they later realized that most of the services access data only through its primary key and they need not use complex queries to fetch the required data, plus maintaining these RDBMS systems required high-end hardware and skilled personnel. So, to overcome all such issues, Amazon's engineering team built a NoSQL database that addresses all the previously mentioned issues.

In 2007, Amazon released one research paper on Dynamo that combined the best of ideas from the database and key-value store worlds, which was inspiration for many open source projects at the time. Cassandra, Voldemort, and Riak were a few of them. You can find the this paper at `http://www.allthingsdistributed.com/files/amazon-dynamo-sosp2007.pdf`.

Even though Dynamo had great features that took care of all engineering needs, it was not widely accepted at that time in Amazon, as it was not a fully managed service. When Amazon released S3 and SimpleDB, engineering teams were quite excited to adopt these compared to Dynamo, as DynamoDB was a bit expensive at that time due to SSDs. So, finally after rounds of improvement, Amazon released Dynamo as a cloud-based service, and since then, it is one the most widely used NoSQL databases.

Before releasing to a public cloud in 2012, DynamoDB was the core storage service for Amazon's e-commerce platform, which started the shopping cart and session management service. Any downtime or degradation in performance had a major impact on Amazon's business, and any financial impact was strictly not acceptable, and DynamoDB proved itself to be the best choice in the end. Now, let's try to understand in more detail about DynamoDB.

What is DynamoDB?

DynamoDB is a fully managed, Internet scalable, easily administered, and cost effective NoSQL database. It is a part of database as a service-offering pane of Amazon Web Services.

The next diagram shows how Amazon offers its various cloud services and where DynamoDB is exactly placed. AWS RDS is a relational database as a service over the Internet from Amazon, while Simple DB and DynamoDB are NoSQL databases as services. Both SimpleDB and DynamoDB are fully managed, nonrelational services. DynamoDB is build considering fast, seamless scalability, and high performance. It runs on SSDs to provide faster responses and has no limits on request capacity and storage. It automatically partitions your data throughout the cluster to meet expectations, while in SimpleDB, we have a storage limit of 10 GB and can only take limited requests per second.

Also, in SimpleDB, we have to manage our own partitions. So, depending upon your need, you have to choose the correct solution.

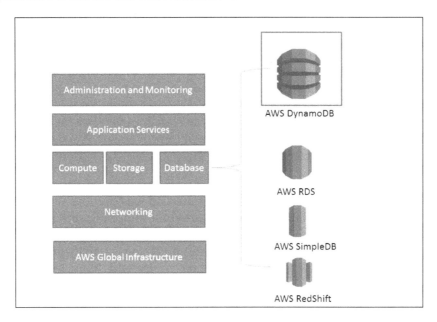

To use DynamoDB, the first and foremost requirement is an AWS account. Through the easy-to-use AWS management console, you can directly create new tables, providing necessary information and can start loading data into the tables in few minutes.

Data model concepts

To understand DynamoDB better, we need to understand its data model first. DynamoDB's data model includes **Tables**, **Items**, and **Attributes**. A table in DynamoDB is nothing but what we have in relational databases. DynamoDB tables need not have fixed schema (number of columns, column names, their data types, column order, and column size). It needs only the fixed primary key, its data type, and a secondary index if needed, and the remaining attributes can be decided at runtime. Items in DynamoDB are individual records of the table. We can have any number of attributes in an item.

DynamoDB stores the item attributes as key-value pairs. Item size is calculated by adding the length of attribute names and their values.

DynamoDB has an item-size limit of 64 KB; so, while designing your data model, you have to keep this thing in mind that your item size must not cross this limitation. There are various ways of avoiding the over spill, and we will discuss such best practices in *Chapter 4, Best Practices*.

The following diagram shows the data model hierarchy of DynamoDB:

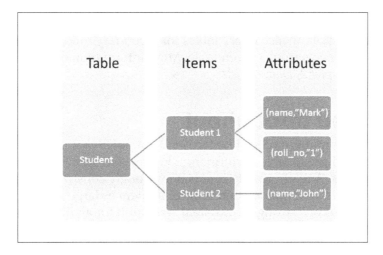

Here, we have a table called **Student**, which can have multiple items in it. Each item can have multiple attributes that are stored in key–value pairs. We will see more details about the data models in *Chapter 2, Data Models*.

Operations

DynamoDB supports various operations to play with tables, items, and attributes.

Table operations

DynamoDB supports the create, update, and delete operations at the table level. It also supports the UpdateTable operation, which can be used to increase or decrease the provisioned throughput. We have the ListTables operation to get the list of all available tables associated with your account for a specific endpoint. The DescribeTable operation can be used to get detailed information about the given table.

Item operations

Item operations allows you to add, update, or delete an item from the given table. The UpdateItem operation allows us to add, update, or delete existing attributes from a given item.

The Query and Scan operations

The Query and Scan operations are used to retrieve information from tables. The Query operation allows us to query the given table with provided hash key and range key. We can also query tables for secondary indexes. The Scan operation reads all items from a given table. More information on operations can be found in *Chapter 2, Data Models*.

Provisioned throughput

Provisioned throughput is a special feature of DynamoDB that allows us to have consistent and predictable performance. We need to specify the read and write capacity units. A read capacity unit is one strongly consistent read and two eventually consistent reads per second unit for an item as large as 4 KB, whereas one write capacity unit is one strongly consistent write unit for an item as large as 1 KB. A consistent read reflects all successful writes prior to that read request, whereas a consistent write updates all replications of a given data object so that a read on this object after this write will always reflect the same value.

For items whose size is more than 4 KB, the required read capacity units are calculated by summing it up to the next closest multiple of 4. For example, if we want to read an item whose size is 11 KB, then the number of read capacity units required is three, as the nearest multiple of 4 to 11 is 12. So, *12/4 = 3* is the required number of read capacity units.

Required Capacity Units For	Consistency	Formula
Reads	Strongly consistent	No. of Item reads per second * Item Size
Reads	Eventually consistent	Number of Item reads per second * Item Size/2
Writes	NA	Number of Item writes per second * Item Size

If our application exceeds the maximum provisioned throughput for a given table, then we get notified with a proper exception. We can also monitor the provisioned and actual throughput from the AWS management console, which will give us the exact idea of our application behavior. To understand it better, let's take an example. Suppose, we have set the write capacity units to 100 for a certain table and if your application starts writing to the table by 1,500 capacity units, then DynamoDB allows the first 1,000 writes and throttles the rest. As all DynamoDB operations work as RESTful services, it gives the error code 400 (Bad Request).

If you have items smaller than 4 KB, even then it will consider it to be a single read capacity unit. We cannot group together multiple items smaller than 4 KB into a single read capacity unit. For instance, if your item size is 3 KB and if you want to read 50 items per second, then you need to provision 50 read capacity units in a table definition for strong consistency and 25 read capacity units for eventual consistency.

If you have items larger than 4 KB, then you have to round up the size to the next multiple of 4. For example, if your item size is 7 KB (~8KB) and you need to read 100 items per second, then the required read capacity units would be 200 for strong consistency and 100 capacity units for eventual consistency.

In the case of write capacity units, the same logic is followed. If the item size is less than 1 KB, then it is rounded up to 1 KB, and if item size is more than 1 KB, then it is rounded up to next multiple of 1.

The AWS SDK provides auto-retries on `ProvisionedThroughputExceededException` when configured though client configuration. This configuration option allows us to set the maximum number of times `HttpClient` should retry sending the request to DynamoDB. It also implements the default backoff strategy that decides the retry interval.

The following is a sample code to set a maximum of three auto retries:

```
    // Create a configuration object
final ClientConfiguration cfg = new ClientConfiguration();
// Set the maximum auto-reties to 3
cfg.setMaxErrorRetry(3);
    // Set configuration object in Client
client.setConfiguration(cfg);
```

DynamoDB features

Like we said earlier, DynamoDB comes with enormous scalability and high availability with predictable performance, which makes it stand out strong compared to other NoSQL databases. It has tons of features; we will discuss some of them.

Fully managed

DynamoDB allows developers to focus on the development part rather than deciding which hardware to provision, how to do administration, how to set up the distributed cluster, how to take care of fault tolerance, and so on. DynamoDB handles all scaling needs; it partitions your data in such a manner that the performance requirements get taken care of. Any distributed system that starts scaling is an overhead to manage but DynamoDB is a fully managed service, so you don't need to bother about hiring an administrator to take care of this system.

Durable

Once data is loaded into DynamoDB, it automatically replicates the data into different availability zones in a region. So, even if your data from one data center gets lost, there is always a backup in another data center. DynamoDB does this automatically and synchronously. By default, DynamoDB replicates your data to three different data centers.

Scalable

DynamoDB distributes your data on multiple servers across multiple availability zones automatically as the data size grows. The number of servers could be easily from hundreds to thousands. Developers can easily write and read data of any size and there are no limitations on data size. DynamoDB follows the shared-nothing architecture.

Fast

DynamoDB serves at a very high throughput, providing single-digit millisecond latency. It uses SSD for consistent and optimized performance at a very high scale. DynamoDB does not index all attributes of a table, saving costs, as it only needs to index the primary key, and this makes read and write operations superfast. Any application running on an EC2 instance will show single-digit millisecond latency for an item of size 1 KB. The latencies remain constant even at scale due to the highly distributed nature and optimized routing algorithms.

Simple administration

DynamoDB is very easy to manage. The Amazon web console has a user-friendly interface to create tables and provide necessary details. You can simply start using the table within a few minutes. Once the data load starts, you don't need to do anything as rest is taken care by DynamoDB. You can monitor Amazon CloudWatch for the provision throughput and can make changes to read and write capacity units accordingly if needed.

Fault tolerance

DynamoDB automatically replicates the data to multiple availability zones which helps in reducing any risk associated with failures.

Flexible

DynamoDB, being a NoSQL database, does not force users to define the table schema beforehand. Being a key-value data store, it allows users to decide what attributes need to be there in an item, on the fly. Each item of a table can have different number of attributes.

Rich Data ModelDynamoDB has a rich data model, which allows a user to define the attributes with various data types, for example, number, string, binary, number set, string set, and binary set. We are going to talk about these data types in *Chapter 2, Data Models*, in detail.

Indexing

DynamoDB indexes the primary key of each item, which allows us to access any element in a faster and efficient manner. It also allows global and local secondary indexes, which allows the user to query on any non-primary key attribute.

Secure

Each call to DynamoDB makes sure that only authenticated users can access the data. It also uses the latest and effective cryptographic techniques to see your data. It can be easily integrated with AWS **Identity and Access Management (IAM)**, which allows users to set fine-grained access control and authorization.

Cost effective

DynamoDB provides a very cost-effective pricing model to host an application of any scale. The pay-per-use model gives users the flexibility to control expenditure. It also provides free tier, which allows users 100 MB free data storage with 5 writes/ second and 10 reads/second as throughput capacity. More details about pricing can be found at `http://aws.amazon.com/dynamodb/pricing/`.

How do I get started?

Now that you are aware of all the exciting features of DynamoDB, I am sure you are itching to try out your hands on it. So let's try to create a table using the Amazon DynamoDB management console. The pre-requisite to do this exercise is having a valid Amazon account and a valid credit card for billing purposes. Once the account is active and you have signed up for the DynamoDB service, you can get started directly. If you are new to AWS, more information is available at `http://docs.aws. amazon.com/gettingstarted/latest/awsgsg-intro/gsg-aws-intro.html`.

Amazon's infrastructure is spread across almost 10 regions worldwide and DynamoDB is available in almost all regions. You can check out more details about it at `https://aws.amazon.com/about-aws/globalinfrastructure/ regional-product-services/`.

Creating a DynamoDB table using the AWS management console

Perform the following steps to create a DynamoDB table using the AWS management console:

1. Go to the Amazon DynamoDB management console at `https://console. aws.amazon.com/dynamodb`, and you will get the following screenshot:

2. Click on the **Create Table** button and you will see a pop-up window asking for various text inputs. Here, we are creating a table called `Employee` having `emp_id` as the hash key and `email` as the range key, as shown in the following screenshot:

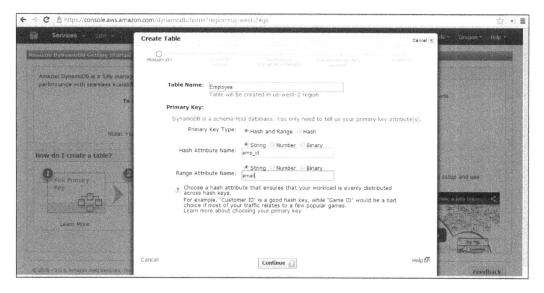

3. Once you click on the **Continue** button, you will see the next window asking to create indexes, as shown in the next screenshot. These are optional parameters; so, if you do not wish to create any secondary indexes, you can skip this and click on **Continue**. We are going to talk about the indexes in *Chapter 2, Data Models*.

4. Once you click on the **Continue** button again, the next page will appear asking for provision throughput capacity units. We have already talked about the read and write capacity; so, depending upon your application requirements, you can give the read and write capacity units in the appropriate text box, as shown in the following screenshot:

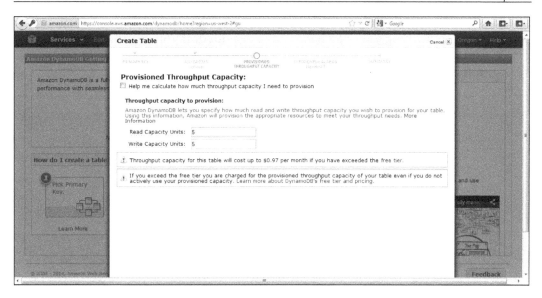

5. The next page will ask whether you want to set any throughput alarm notifications for this particular table. You can provide an e-mail ID on which you wish to get the alarms, as shown in the following screenshot. If not, you can simply skip it.

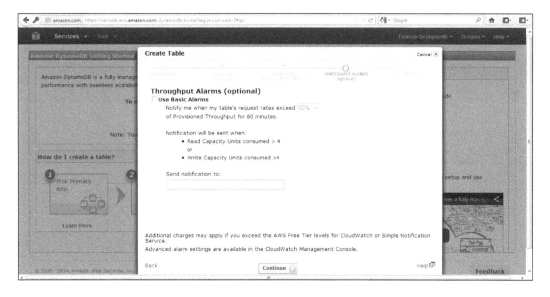

6. Once you set the required alarms, the next page would be a summary page confirming the details you have provided. If you see all the given details are correct, you can click on the **Create** button, as shown in the following screenshot:

7. Once the **Create** button is clicked, Amazon starts provisioning the hardware and other logistics in the background and takes a couple of minutes to create the table. In the meantime, you can see the table creations status as **CREATING** on the screen, as shown in the following screenshot:

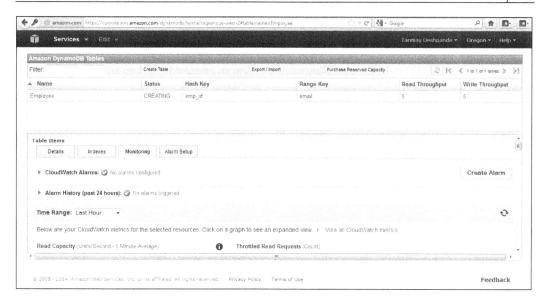

8. Once the table is created, you can see the status changed to **ACTIVE** on the screen, as shown in the following screenshot:

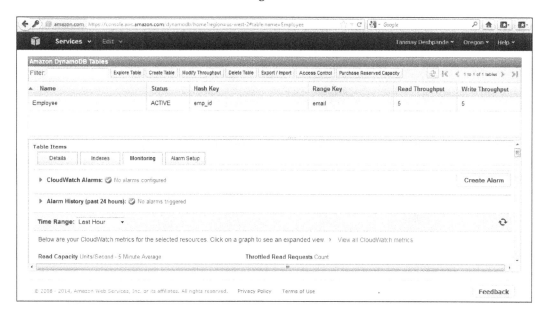

9. Now that the table `Employee` is created and active, let's try to put an item in it. Once you double-click on the **Explore Table** button, you will see the following screen:

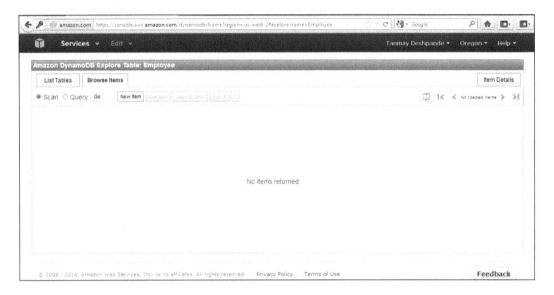

10. You can click on the **New Item** button to add a new record to the table, which will open up a pop up asking for various attributes that we wish to add in this record. Earlier, we had added `emp_id` and `email` as hash and range key, respectively. These are mandatory attributes we have to provide with some optional attributes if you want to, as shown in the following screenshot:

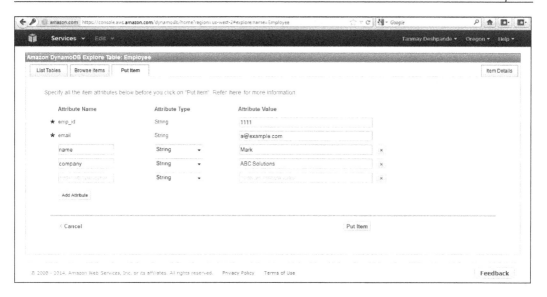

Here, I have added two extra attributes, name and company, with some relevant values. Once done, you can click on the **Put Item** button to actually add the item to the table.

11. You can go to the **Browse Items** tab to see whether the item has been added. You can select **Scan** to list down all items in the Employee table, which is shown in the following screenshot:

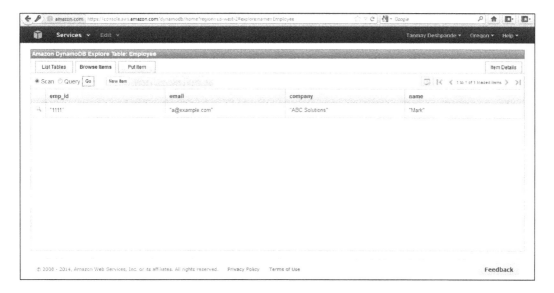

In *Chapter 2*, *Data Models*, we will be looking for various examples in Java, .Net, and PHP to play around with tables, items, and attributes.

DynamoDB Local

DynamoDB is a lightweight client-side database that mimics the actual DynamoDB database. It enables users to develop and test their code in house, without consuming actual DynamoDB resources. DynamoDB Local supports all DynamoDB APIs, with which you can run your code like running on an actual DynamoDB.

To use DynamoDB Local, you need to run a Java service on the desired port and direct your calls from code to this service. Once you try to test your code, you can simply redirect it to an actual DynamoDB.

So, using this, you can code your application without having full Internet connectivity all the time, and once you are ready to deploy your application, simply make a single line change to point your code to an actual DynamoDB and that's it.

Installing and running DynamoDB Local is quite easy and quick; you just have to perform the following steps and you can get started with it:

1. Download the DynamoDB Local executable JAR, which can be run on Windows, Mac, or Linux. You can download this JAR file from `http://dynamodb-local.s3-website-us-west-2.amazonaws.com/dynamodb_local_latest`.

2. This JAR file is compiled on version 7 of JRE, so it might not be suitable to run on the older JRE version.

3. The given ZIP file contains two important things: a `DynamoDBLocal_lib` folder that contains various third-party JAR files that are being used, and `DynamoDBLocal.jar` which contains the actual entry point.

4. Once you unzip the file, simply run the following command to get started with the local instance:

   ```
   java -Djava.library.path=. -jar DynamoDBLocal.jar
   ```

5. Once you press *Enter*, the DynamoDB Local instance gets started, as shown in the following screenshot:

By default, the DynamoDB Local service runs on port 8000.

6. In case you are using port 8000 for some other service, you can simply choose your own port number by running the following command:

```
java -Djava.library.path=. -jar DynamoDBLocal.jar --port
<YourPortNumber>
```

Now, let's see how to use DynamoDB Local in the Java API. The complete implementation remains the same; the only thing that we need to do is set the endpoint in the client configuration as `http://localhost:8000`.

Using DynamoDB for development in Java is quite easy; you just need to set the previous URL as the endpoint while creating DynamoDB Client, as shown in the following code:

```
// Instantiate AWS Client with proper credentials
AmazonDynamoDBClient dynamoDBClient = new AmazonDynamoDBClient(
  new ClasspathPropertiesFileCredentialsProvider());
Region usWest2 = Region.getRegion(Regions.US_WEST_2);
  dynamoDBClient.setRegion(usWest2);
// Set DynamoDB Local Endpoint
  dynamoDBClient.setEndpoint("http://localhost:8000");
```

Once you are comfortable with your development and you are ready to use the actual DynamoDB, simply remove the highlighted line from the previous code snippet and you are done. Everything will work as expected.

DynamoDB Local is useful but before using it, we should make a note of following things:

- DynamoDB Local ignores the credentials you have provided.

- The values provided in the access key and regions are used to create only the local database file. The DB file gets created in the same folder from where you are running your DynamoDB Local.

- DynamoDB Local ignores the settings provided for provision throughput. So, even if you specify the same at table creation, it will simply ignore it. It does not prepare you to handle provision throughput exceeded exceptions, so you need to be cautious about handling it in production.

- Last but not least, DynamoDB Local is meant to be used for development and unit testing purposes only and should not be used for production purposes, as it does not have durability or availability SLAs.

Summary

In this chapter, we talked about DynamoDB's history, its features, the concept of provision throughput, and why it is important from the DynamoDB usage point of view. We also saw how you can get started with AWS DynamoDB and create a table and load data. We also learned about installing and running a DynamoDB Local instance utility and how to use it for development.

In the next chapter, we will discuss the DynamoDB data model in more detail and how to use DynamoDB APIs to perform the table, item, and attribute level operations.

2
Data Models

The flexibility of any database depends on the architecture and design of its data models. A data model fundamentally decides how data is stored, organized, and can be manipulated. When it comes to typical a RDBMS, we tend to provide the information in terms of hierarchical, relational, and network data models. SQL was designed to interact with an end user assuming he/she will use SQL to run queries that would aggregate data at one place, giving all information together. But it takes a lot of effort to maintain this user-oriented approach. Later, people realized that most of the time is being spent on creating database schemas, maintaining referential integrity, and providing transactional guarantees even though they are not using these things much. This thought ultimately resulted in the implementation of schema-less, relation-free databases, that is, NoSQL databases.

Relational data modeling starts with all the data that you have and the answers you can provide with data, whereas NoSQL data modeling is application oriented. Here, we create tables and decide on our columns, which directly solves the application-specific problem. NoSQL data modeling requires better understanding of the problem that you are trying to solve with your application.

In the previous chapter, we have seen a glimpse of DynamoDB data models. There, we discussed tables, items, and attributes. In this chapter, we are going to talk about how to programmatically create, update, and delete tables, items, and attributes. We are also going to discuss the primary keys used in DynamoDB, intelligently choosing hash and range keys for better performance, and the data types that are available.

For better understanding of DynamoDB, we have divided this chapter into the following parts:

- Primary keys
- Data types
- Operations

Just to understand in a better manner, let's see what tables, items, and attributes look like.

Consider an example of a bookstore where we have multiple entities, such as Books, Authors, and Publishers, and so on. So, to understand the DynamoDB data model in a better way, please have a look at the following diagram that shows how a Book table would look:

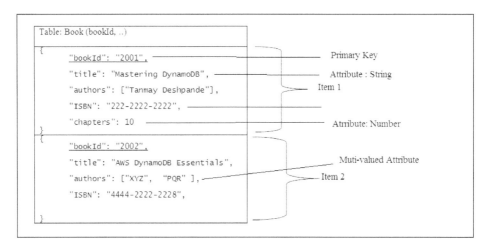

Here, we have chosen a BookId field as the primary key on which the complete item would get indexed. We have also included a couple of sample items that have multiple attributes. Some of them have string as their data type, some have number, whereas some others are multivalued attributes. You can also observe that the number of attributes in given items need not be the same. The first item has the chapters attribute, while the second item does not have it. This is because we don't have *strict* schema in NoSQL databases.

Also, both the items have bookId as the primary key, which needs to be unique for each attribute. Now let's try to understand more about primary keys in DynamoDB.

Primary key

DynamoDB, being a key-value pair database, does not index on all given attributes for a given item; it only indexes on the primary key, which is a mandatory attribute for each item of the table.

DynamoDB supports two types of primary keys:

- Hash primary key
- Hash and range primary key

Hash primary key

Each DynamoDB table must have a hash primary key that is unique for each item. DynamoDB builds an unordered hash index on this key that allows us to uniquely identify any given item for a given table. So, while designing your table, you must choose an attribute that would have a unique value for each attribute. For example, while creating `Person` table, choosing **Social Security Number** (**SSN**) as a hash key would be a better option as compared to selecting a person's name as hash key, as there might be more than one person having the same name.

Hash and range primary key

Along with the hash key, DynamoDB also supports another primary key called range key, which can be used in combination with the hash key. In this case, DynamoDB created an unordered hash index on the hash key and sorted the range key index on a range key attribute. Range key should be selected in such a manner that it will evenly distribute the data load across partitions.

A good example to choose a hash and range type primary key for the `Person` table would be choosing birth years as the hash key and SSN as the range key. Here, we can narrow down our search with the birth year and then search in a specific birth year range partition for a specific SSN.

> In general, the **hash index** is a set of buckets identified by a certain hash value. The hash value is calculated by some function that is robust and gives the same results on multiple executions. The hashing algorithm decides what value gets emitted for a given key. The simplest example of hash algorithms is the Modulo 10 function: $f(x) = x\ Modulo\ 10$. Here, x is a key. So, if we use this hashing algorithm for indexing and a key has a value, say 17, it would emit the hash value as 17 Modulo 10 = 7.
>
> **Range index** is a special type of index that helps align the set of data into a certain range, which helps in faster retrieval of the given item. When we implement the range index on a certain attribute, we create n number of slots on that data. Consider we have five slots for a given set of data starting from key value 1 to 100, then slots get created from 1-20, 21-40,..., and 81-100.

Now let's redefine our bookstore schema and see when to use the hash key and when to use the composite hash and range keys. We can consider the following primary key specifications for the given tables:

Table name	Primary key type	Hash key	Range key
Book (yearOfPublishing, bookId, , ..)	Hash key and range	yearOfPublishing— this will allow us to save books as per the year in which they got published	bookId— unique book ID
Author (authorId,..)	Hash key	authorId—unique author ID	NA
Publisher (publisherId,..)	Hash key	publisherId—unique publisher ID	NA

So, here it makes sense to use the composite hash and range key for the Book table, which will allow us to have balanced books data depending on their year of publishing. As we don't have many ranges for the Author and Publisher table, so here we have opted for only the hash key.

After the redesign, sample Book items would look like the following screenshot:

Book (yearOfPublication, bookId)

```
{
        "yearOfPublication": "2014",
        "bookId": "2001",
        "title": "Mastering DynamoDB",
        "authors": ["Tanmay Deshpande"],
        "ISBN": "222-222-222",
        "chapters": 10
}

{
        "yearOfPublication": "2014",
        "bookId": "2002",
        "title": "Mastering AWS EMR",
        "authors": ["XYZ", "PQR"],
        "ISBN": "222-222-888",
        "chapters": 9
}
```

Secondary indexes

A primary key attribute allows us to create, maintain, and access data efficiently. To do so, DynamoDB creates indexes on those primary attributes as we have seen in the previous section. However, sometimes there might be a need to search and access items from attributes that are not part of the primary key. For all such needs, DynamoDB supports secondary indexes that can be created on attributes other than the primary key and can be accessed and searched in a manner similar to the primary key.

A secondary index contains a subset of attributes from the given table having an alternative key to support query operations. Secondary index allows users to search attributes other than the primary key, which makes DynamoDB useful for a varied set of applications. We can create multiple secondary indexes for a given table. If we don't create secondary indexes, the only option to get the item for a certain non-primary key attribute is to scan the complete table, which is a very expensive operation.

Internally, when you create a secondary index, you have to specify the attributes to be projected or included as part of the secondary index. DynamoDB copies those attributes to the index. Querying a secondary index is similar to querying a table with the hash and range key. You have to specify the hash key and the optional range for every new index that you create. These secondary indexes are maintained by DynamoDB itself, so if we can add, modify, or delete indexed attributes, it gets reflected on the index as well. One thing to note here is that you need to create secondary indexes at the time of table creation itself, and you cannot add indexes to already existing tables. Also, DynamoDB does not allow editing or deleting indexes from a given table.

DynamoDB supports two types of secondary indexes:

- Local secondary index
- Global secondary index

Local secondary index

Local secondary indexes are nothing but extensions to the given hash and range key attributes. Suppose you have a `Blog` table that keeps track of all posts from different users. Here, we have a hash key, say, `username`, and a range key, say, `date of post`. So you can create a local secondary index on the `topic` attribute that would allow you to fetch all blogs on a particular topic by a given user.

Basically, local secondary indexes give you more range query options other than your table range key attribute. So to define the local secondary index, we can say that it is an index which has the same hash key as a table but a different range key.

Some important points to note about local secondary indexes are as follows:

- A local secondary index must have both hash and range keys.

- The hash key of the local secondary index is the same as that of the table.

- The local secondary index allows you to query data from a single partition only, which is specified by a hash key. As we know DynamoDB creates partitions for unique hash values, the local secondary index allows us to query non-key attributes for a specific hash key.

- The local secondary index supports both eventual and strong consistency, so while querying data, you can choose whichever is suitable.

- Queries and writes consume read and write capacity from provisioned throughput for the given table.

- The local secondary index has a size limit of 10 GB on all indexed items per hash key, which means that all indexed items size together should be less than or equal to 10 GB for a single hash key.

- Indexes should be used sparingly, as they add to the total cost of table storage. Also, while choosing projected attributes, one needs to be very careful with selections.

For any item in a DynamoDB table, it will only create an entry in the index if the index range key attribute is present in that item. If the range key attribute does not appear in each and every item of the table, then the index is called a sparse index. For example, you have a table called `Book`, which has an attribute called `bookId` and `isOpenAccess`. Now, you can create a local secondary index choosing `bookId` as the hash key and `isOpenAccess` as the range key; you can set this attribute to true only if the book is open access and you don't need to set any blank or false value if the `Book` table is not open access. This would make this index a sparse index, and DynamoDB would add an entry in the index only if this attribute is present. This would allow you to easily identify all the books that are open access and can easily fetch them and perform operations on them. So it is advised to take advantage of sparse indexes whenever possible for better performance.

Global secondary index

Global secondary indexes are an advancement over local secondary indexes, which allow users to query data from all over the table compared to only a single partition in the case of the local secondary index. To understand the global secondary index better, let's consider the same example that we had discussed earlier for the local secondary index. There, we had created a table called `Blog`, which contains multiple posts from various users having `username` as the hash key and `date of post` as the range key. We created a local secondary index topic that helped us to query all blogs for a particular topic by a given user. But what if I want to query all blogs on a certain topic from all users? This is the exact problem the global secondary index solves.

The global name suggests a query search on all table partitions compared to a single partition in the case of the local secondary index. Here, we can create a new hash key and an optional range key, which is different than the table hash and range keys to get the index working.

Some important points to note about a global secondary index are as follows:

- The global secondary index should have a hash key and an optional range key.
- The hash and range keys of a global secondary index are different from table hash and range keys.
- The global secondary index allows you to query data across the table. It does not restrict its search for a single data partition; hence, the name global.
- The global secondary index eventually supports only consistent reads.
- The global secondary index maintains its separate read and write capacity units, and it does not take read and write capacity units from the table capacity units.
- Unlike the local secondary index, global ones do not have any size limits.

You can also take advantage of sparse indexes as explained in an earlier section. The following table shows the difference between local and global secondary indexes:

Parameter	Local secondary index	Global secondary index
Hash and range keys	Needs both hash and range keys. The index hash key is the same as the table hash key.	Needs hash key and optional range key. Index hash and range keys are different than those of table keys.

Parameter	Local secondary index	Global secondary index
Query scope	Limited to single partition data only.	Queries over complete table data, which means you can also query on other hash keys that are not part of table hash keys.
Consistency	Provides option to select either eventual or strong consistency.	Supports only eventual consistency.
Size	The size of all items together for a single index should be less than 10 GB per hash key.	No size limit.
Provisioned throughput	Uses the same provisioned throughput as specified for a table.	Has a different calculation for provisioned throughput. We need to specify the read and write capacity units at the time of index creation itself.

There is no argument whether the global secondary index is better or the local secondary index. It totally depends upon what use case you have. So if you know the access pattern of your application, it would not take much time to decide which index to use and which one not to.

Data types

DynamoDB supports various data types, broadly classified into the following two types:

- Scalar data types (string, number, and binary)
- Multivalued data types (string set, number set, and binary set)

Scalar data types

Scalar data types are simply single-value, simple data types. DynamoDB supports the following three scalar data types:

- String
- Number
- Binary

String

The string is a multipurpose, useful data type that is similar to what we use in various programming languages. DynamoDB strings support UTF-8 binary encoding. DynamoDB does not put restrictions on the string size limit, but it specifies that the total attribute size should not be greater than 64 KB and we already know that attribute value is calculated considering the attribute name (key) plus attribute value together. When it comes to ordered query results, DynamoDB does the comparison using ASCII character code value, which means smaller letters (a,b,c,...) are greater than capital letters (A,B,C,...). One thing to note here is that DynamoDB does not allow us to store empty strings, so if you don't have any value for an attribute for a certain item, it will not add the attribute itself.

Number

The number in DynamoDB is either positive or negative, and it is either an exact-value decimal or an integer. DynamoDB supports as long as 38-digit precision after decimal point values to be stored as numbers, which means that DynamoDB supports number values ranging between 10^{-128} and 10^{+126}. When numbers are transferred from one place to other, serialized numbers are transformed as strings, which gives the benefit of stronger compatibility between various languages and libraries. But when it comes to mathematical operations, DynamoDB, as expected, treats them as numbers.

Binary

The binary data type in DynamoDB works like **binary large object (BLOBs)** and **character large object (CLOBs)** in the relational database. Once you declare a variable as binary, you can store binary data like zip files, images, XML files, and so on in it. By default, DynamoDB encodes the given data using the Base64 encoder and then stores it in the table. To read back the original binary value, you should decode it using the Base64 decoder.

Sometimes, developers find it difficult to store and retrieve, so the following is the Java code to store binary attributes in DynamoDB:

```
//Convert string representation of XML into byte buffers
ByteBuffer  bb =  ByteBuffer.wrap("<student><name>Tanmay</name></
student>".getBytes());
// Put bookXml attribute key and value into item.
item.put("studentXML", new AttributeValue().withB(bb));
```

So, once you invoke the `put` item request, the values get stored, and the DynamoDB console shows the Base64 encoded value stored in the `bookXML` attribute, as shown in the following screenshot:

To get back the actual value stored in the binary attribute, you can write the following code:

```
String studentDetails = new String( item.get("studentXML").getB().
array(), "UTF-8");
System.out.println(studentDetails);
```

This prints the original string back on the console:

```
<student><name>James Bond</name></student>
```

Multivalued data types

DynamoDB supports complex data types that are formed by using one or more scalar data types. There are three multivalued data types supported by DynamoDB:

- String sets
- Number sets
- Binary sets

In the previous section, we had seen one example of the `Book` table having the `authors` attribute. This `authors` attribute is a good example of a string set. Similarly, number sets and binary sets can also be defined and used. An example of a number set would be the `marks` attribute in a `Student` table, and an example of a binary set would be `images` included in the `Chapter` table.

As these data types are sets, the values in a set must be unique. DynamoDB does not put any order on the attribute values of a set. It also does not support empty sets.

Now, that we have seen primary keys, secondary indexes, and data types in DynamoDB, let's start discussing operations on tables, items, and attributes.

Operations on tables

A table in DynamoDB is quite easy to create and operate. With a few clicks on the DynamoDB management console, you can have your table created in a couple of minutes. To do so, you just need a suitable table name, primary key attributes, their data types, and read and write throughput provisioning units, and you are done. DynamoDB allows us to use the characters a-z, A-Z, 0-9, - (dash), .(dot), and _(underscore) in table names.

We have already seen how to create a table using the AWS management console in the previous chapter. Now, let's try to do table operations using the AWS SDK.

Using the AWS SDK for Java

In this section, we are going to see how to use the AWS SDK for Java to perform operations.

Create table

Before creating a table, you should have thought about how the user is going to use that table in his/her application. Data modeling in DynamoDB should be application oriented in order to get the maximum benefit of the NoSQL features. You should also have a proper idea of the reads and writes you are going to expect for a particular table so that there won't be any `ProvisionedThroughputExceededException` and all request to DynamoDB will be handled properly.

DynamoDB provides the SDK to create, update, and delete tables using a Java API. We can also scan or query a table and get table description using a simple Java API. The following are the steps to create a table in AWS DynamoDB. The SDK includes two versions of APIs, Versions 1 and 2, so make sure that while you are importing packages in Eclipse, you point to `com.amazonaws.services.dynamodbv2` rather than `com.amazonaws.services.dynamodb`. Perform the following steps:

1. Create an instance of `AmazonDynamoDBClient` and initialize it using your AWS credentials, that is, your access key and secret key:

   ```
   AmazonDynamoDBClient dynamoDBClient = new AmazonDynamoDBClient(
           new ClasspathPropertiesFileCredentialsProvider());
   ```

   By default, AWS looks for the `properties` file name `AwsCredentials.properties` in `classpath`, which should have two properties set: `accessKey` and `secretKey`.

2. Create an instance of `CreateTableRequest` and provide information such as table name, key schema, and provision throughput details, as shown in the following code:

```
// Key attribute definition
ArrayList<AttributeDefinition> attrDefList= new ArrayList<Attribut
eDefinition>();
attrDefList.add(new AttributeDefinition().
withAttributeName("bookId").withAttributeType("N"));
attrDefList.add(new AttributeDefinition().
withAttributeName("yop").withAttributeType("S"));

// Define primary key schema

ArrayList<KeySchemaElement> ks = new
ArrayList<KeySchemaElement>();
    ks.add(new KeySchemaElement("bookId", KeyType.HASH));
    ks.add(new KeySchemaElement("yop",KeyType.RANGE));

// Provision throughput settings
ProvisionedThroughput provisionedThroughput = new
ProvisionedThroughput()
      .withReadCapacityUnits(20L)
      .withWriteCapacityUnits(20L);

// Create table request with specifications

CreateTableRequest request = new CreateTableRequest()
      .withTableName("book")
      .withAttributeDefinitions(attrDefList)
      .withKeySchema(ks)
      .withProvisionedThroughput(provisionedThroughput);

// Submit create table request to client
CreateTableResult result = dynamoDBClient.createTable(request);
```

Once the request is submitted, DynamoDB takes a couple of minutes to get the table activated; meanwhile, the SDK provides an API to wait:

```
Tables.waitForTableToBecomeActive(dynamoDBClient, "Book");
```

Once the table is activated, you can continue with further execution.

Update table

To update the already created table, DynamoDB provides the `UpdateTableRequest` API. Here, you just need to specify the table and the table properties you need to update. You can update the provision throughput setting or global secondary index. One thing to note with the API is that it can't be used to add/remove any secondary indexes. The following is the syntax to use:

```
// Create a provision throughput instance with updated read and write
unit values
ProvisionedThroughput updateProvisionedThroughput = new
ProvisionedThroughput()
    .withReadCapacityUnits(30L).withWriteCapacityUnits(30L);
// Create update table request instance and provide the necessary
details
UpdateTableRequest updateTableRequest = new UpdateTableRequest()
        .withTableName("Book")
        .withProvisionedThroughput(updateProvisionedThroughput);
```

Once done, you can call the `updateTable` method from the DynamoDB client:

```
UpdateTableResult result = dynamoDBClient.updateTable(updateTableRequest);
```

Delete table

The AWS SDK allows us to delete a certain table from DynamoDB using the `DeleteTableRequest` API. To delete a table, you just need to specify the table name. Please use this API with care as, once the table is deleted, there is no way to get it back.

```
DeleteTableRequest deleteTableRequest = new DeleteTableRequest()
        .withTableName("Book");
```

Once done, you can invoke the `deleteTable` method from the DynamoDB client, which would execute the request:

```
DeleteTableResult deleteTableResult = dynamoDBClient.deleteTable(deleteTableRequest);
```

Please note that the `delete` table API call will only change the status of the table from Active to Deleting; it may take some time to completely remove that table. Once it is done, you can create a DynamoDB table with the same name.

List tables

DynamoDB gives us an API to list down all the tables currently associated with a particular account. You can invoke the `listTable` method from the DynamoDB client to get the complete list. It also allows us to provide optional parameters if we wish to see pagination. You can also limit the results to a specific number as shown in the following code snippet. You can also specify if you want DynamoDB to start evaluating this request from a specific table. Have a look at the following code:

```
ListTablesRequest listTablesRequest = new ListTablesRequest()
        .withLimit(5).withExclusiveStartTableName("Book");
ListTablesResult listTablesResult = dynamoDBClient.
listTables(listTablesRequest);
```

The `ListTablesResult` function gives methods, such as `getTableNames` and `getLastEvaluatedTableName`, to provide more details.

Using the AWS SDK for .NET

Like Java, AWS also provides an SDK for .NET and PHP development. The following are some examples that show how to create, update, delete, and list tables using .NET.

Create table

To perform any operation in .NET, we need to create an instance of the DynamoDB client first:

```
var configuration = new AmazonDynamoDBConfig();
configuration.ServiceURL = System.Configuration.ConfigurationManager.
AppSettings["ServiceURL"];
dynamoDBClient = new AmazonDynamoDBClient(configuration);
Once the client is ready, you can build a create table request and
invoke the same using dynamoDBClient
var createTableRequest = new CreateTableRequest
    {
    // Create Attribute definition
        AttributeDefinitions = new List<AttributeDefinition>()
        { new AttributeDefinition {
            AttributeName = "bookId",
            AttributeType = "N"
          },
          new AttributeDefinition
          {
            AttributeName = "yop",
```

```
                AttributeType = "N"
            }
        },
    // Create primary key schema
        KeySchema = new List<KeySchemaElement>
        {
          new KeySchemaElement
          {
            AttributeName = "bookId",
            KeyType = "HASH"
          },
          new KeySchemaElement
          {
            AttributeName = "yop",
            KeyType = "RANGE"
          }
        },
    // Create provision throughput settings
        ProvisionedThroughput = new ProvisionedThroughput
        {
          ReadCapacityUnits = 10,
          WriteCapacityUnits = 10
        },
        TableName = "Book"
      };

// Invoke CreateTable method
var response = dynamoDBClient.CreateTable(createTableRequest);
```

Update table

Just like creating a table, you can also update the already created table; DynamoDB allows us to only update the provision throughput and global secondary index configurations:

```
// Create instance of updateTableRequest

    var udpateTableRequest = new UpdateTableRequest()
    {
      TableName = "Book",

// Create provision throughput instance with updated read and write
units
```

```
    ProvisionedThroughput = new ProvisionedThroughput()
    {
      ReadCapacityUnits = 30,
      WriteCapacityUnits = 30
    }
  };
// Invoke UpdateTable method of dynamodb client
  var response = dynamoDBClient.UpdateTable(udpateTableRequest);
```

Delete table

The delete table request is quite invoke. `DeleteTableRequest` only needs the name of the table to be deleted and you are done. Note that a table once deleted cannot be retrieved, so handle this API with care. Have a look at the following code:

```
var deleteTableRequest = new DeleteTableRequest
    {
      TableName = "Book"
    };

var response = client.DeleteTable(deleteTableRequest);
```

List tables

This method allows us to list down all available tables for a given account. You can optionally also mention whether you want to restrict the list to a specified number. Also, you can mention whether you want DynamoDB to start the evaluation from a particular table. Have a look at the following code:

```
var listTableRequest = new ListTablesRequest
      {
        Limit = 10,
        ExclusiveStartTableName = "Authors"
      };

var response = dynamoDBClient.ListTables(listTableRequest);
```

Using the AWS SDK for PHP

AWS has also given an SDK for PHP, with which you can perform table operations such as create, update, delete, and list tables. Let's try to understand the implementation in greater detail.

Create table

You can create a DynamoDB table in PHP by providing information, such as table name, provision throughput settings, attributes, and primary key schema.

To invoke any table operation, first you need to create an instance of the DynamoDB client and instantiate it with your AWS credentials, as shown in the following code:

```php
$aws = Aws\Common\Aws::factory("./config.php");
$dynamodclient = $aws->get("dynamodb");
Once done, you can form create table request by providing required
details.
$tableName = "Book";

$result = $ dynamodclient ->createTable(array(
    "TableName" => $tableName,
    "AttributeDefinitions" => array(
        array(
            "AttributeName" => "bookId",
            "AttributeType" => Type::NUMBER
        )
    ),
    "KeySchema" => array(
        array(
            "AttributeName" => "bookId",
            "KeyType" => KeyType::HASH
        )
    ),
    "ProvisionedThroughput" => array(
        "ReadCapacityUnits"  => 10,
        "WriteCapacityUnits" => 10
    )
));
```

This creates a table on DynamoDB and can be used to store data once active.

Update table

Updating a table in DynamoDB is quite easy; you just need to specify the table name and the specifications that need to be updated. DynamoDB allows us to only update provision throughput configurations and the global secondary index. The following is an example of this:

```php
$tableName = "Book";


$dynamodbclient->updateTable(array(
```

```
      "TableName" => $tableName,
      "ProvisionedThroughput"    => array(
          "ReadCapacityUnits"    => 30,
          "WriteCapacityUnits" => 30
      )
));
```

Here we are updating the read and write capacity units to 30 for the table `Book`.

Delete table

Deleting a table in DynamoDB is quite easy; you just need to mention the name of the table to be deleted and invoke the `deleteTable` method. You should be careful while using this API as a table, once deleted, cannot be retrieved back.

```
$tableName = "Book";


$result = $dynamodbclient->deleteTable(array(
    "TableName" => $tableName
));
```

List tables

The DynamoDB SDK allows us to list down all available tables for a given account by invoking the `listtable` method from the DynamoDB client. You can optionally mention whether you want to limit the result to a specific number. You can also mention whether you want DynamoDB to start the evaluation from a particular table. The following is the code to perform the same:

```
$response = $dynamodbclient ->listTables(array(
        'Limit' => 10,
        'ExclusiveStartTableName' => isset($response) ? $response['Las
tEvaluatedTableName'] : null
    ));
```

Operations on items

Items in DynamoDB are simply collections of attributes. Attributes can be in the form of strings, numbers, binaries, or a set of scalar attributes. Each attribute consists of a name and a value. An item must have a primary key. As we have already seen, a primary key can have a hash key or a combination of hash and range keys. In addition to the primary key, items can have any number of attributes except for the fact that item size cannot exceed 64 KB.

While doing various item operations, you should have be aware of following DynamoDB features.

Strong versus eventual consistency

In *Chapter 1*, *Getting Started*, we had talked about the durability feature of DynamoDB. To provide this durability, DynamoDB keep copies of items in various availability zones. When a certain item gets updated, DynamoDB needs to make sure that it updates all other copies as well. However, it takes time to make any write consistent on all servers; that's why the operation is called eventually consistent. DynamoDB also supports strong consistency where it provides you with the latest updated copy of any item, but it takes more read capacity units to perform this operation. Eventually consistent reads are lightweight and take only half the read capacity units to perform the operation when compared with strong consistent reads.

So, in order to make the most of DynamoDB, it's very important to design your application in such a manner that eventually consistent reads can be used whenever possible to increase the time and cost efficiency.

Before you decide to use eventually consistent reads, you should ask yourself the following questions:

- Can my item operation tolerate stale reads?
- Can it tolerate out-of-order values?
- Can it tolerate returning some other values updated by someone else after my update?

Eventual consistency

Eventual consistency is a special type of weak consistency, where the system guarantees to return the last updated values to all clients eventually. In distributed systems, to improve the read and write performance, you have to tolerate the data inconsistency under highly concurrent reads and writes. There are various types of eventual consistency:

- **Casual**: Consider that client 1 has updated a data item and has notified the same to client 2, then a subsequent operation by client 2 will guarantee the return of the most updated data. Meanwhile, if client 3 performs any operation on the same data item, and clients 1 and 3 do not have any casual relation, then the data will be returned based on the sequence of performance.
- **Read-your-writes**: In this case if client 1 has updated a certain value, then it will always access the updated value.

- **Session**: In this eventual consistency model, if a session has updated a certain value, then as long as a session is alive, it will always get the most updated value.

These types need not be put in all at once. One thing to note here is that eventual consistency is not a NoSQL proprietary; most of the legacy RDBMSes also use the eventual consistency model in order to improve performance.

Conditional writes

Conditional writes are a special feature of DynamoDB designed to avoid data inconsistency when it updates multiple users at the same time. There might be a case where two clients read a certain data item at the same time, and if client 1 updates it first, and then client 2 updates it again, the update by client 1 would be lost. Let's understand this scenario in detail.

Consider that we have a `book` table that contains an attribute called `bookPrice`. Now, if two clients are trying to increase the price by some amount, then there might be a chance that the update that was done to the item first would be lost, as shown in the following diagram:

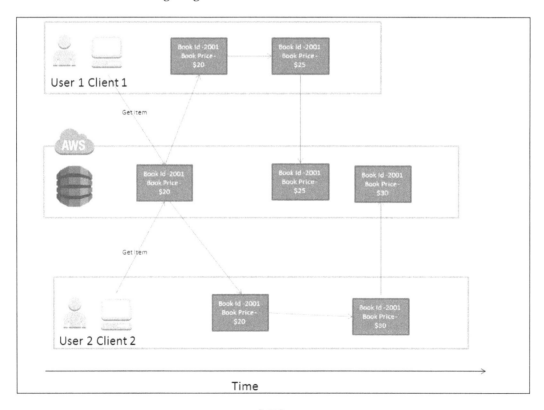

In this case, updates made by client 1 are lost. In order to avoid this, DynamoDB provides the conditional write feature, which allows the updates only if certain conditions are fulfilled. In this, we can put a condition such as update the book price only if the current book price is $20. If that is not the case, then DynamoDB will fail that operation and give the necessary feedback to the client, as shown in the following diagram:

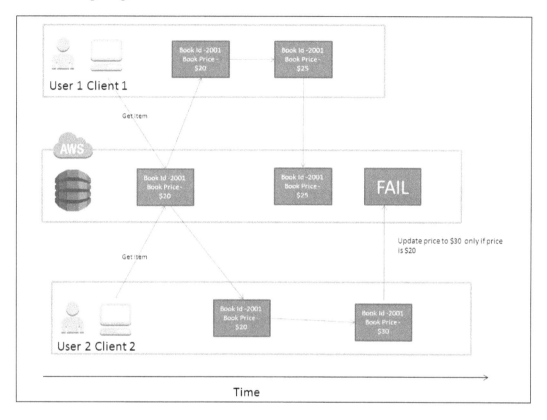

There might be multiple use cases where conditional writes can be useful. Suppose you are working on some transaction data where data consistency is extremely critical, then you can use conditional writes to avoid missed updates.

AWS supports **atomic counters**, which can be used to increment or decrement the value as and when needed. This is a special feature that handles the data increment and decrement request in the order they are received. To implement atomic counters, you can use the ADD operation of the UpdateItem API. A good use case to implement atomic counters is website visitor count. So, in this case, the request will keep updating the attribute by one regardless of its current or previous value. Atomic counters are not idempotent, which means the counter value would get updated even if the request fails, so it does not guarantee accuracy of count. So it is advisable to use atomic counters only where a slight overcalculation or undercalculation of value is acceptable and should not be used where getting the correct count is critical. So using atomic counters for the website visitor counter is good, but it is not advisable to use them for any banking operation.

Item size calculations

Item size in DynamoDB is calculated by adding all attributes' names and their respective values. In *Chapter 1, Getting Started*, we have seen how read and write capacity units are calculated, where we said that each read operation of DynamoDB is of size 4 KB and each write operation of 1 KB. So it makes sense to design the attributes in such a manner that each read request should get the data size which is a multiple of 4 KB, as even if you read 3 KB, DynamoDB would round it up to 4 KB; the same is the case for write operations, which should write the data in multiples of 1 KB.

In order to optimize the read and write capacity units, you should try to reduce the item size. One good practice to reduce the item size is to reduce the size of the attribute name/length. For example, instead of having the attribute name as yearOfPublishing, you should use the acronym yop.

Now that we have understood special features of Items in DynamoDB, let's learn how to manipulate items using the AWS SDK using Java, .NET, and PHP APIs.

Using the AWS SDK for Java

Earlier in this section, we saw how to manipulate tables using the Java API; now, let's learn how to manipulate items from a certain table.

Put item

This method allows us to store an item in a DynamoDB table. To put the item in the DynamoDB table, you just need to create `PutItemRequest` and call the `putItem` method with the provided details. To call the `putItem` method, you should first initialize the DynamoDB client, which we have already seen in the *Table operations* section, as shown in the following code:

```
AmazonDynamoDBClient dynamoDBClient = new AmazonDynamoDBClient(
        new ClasspathPropertiesFileCredentialsProvider());

// Create Map of String and AttributeValue and store the data in it.
Map<String, AttributeValue> item = new HashMap<String,
AttributeValue>();
    item.put("bookId", new AttributeValue().withN("2001"));
    item.put("name", new AttributeValue().withS("Mastering DynamoDB"));
    item.put("isbn", new AttributeValue().withS("2222-222-222"));
    item.put("authors", new AttributeValue().withSS(Arrays.
asList("Tanmay Deshpande")));

// Initiate with PutItemRequest with table name and item to be added
PutItemRequest putItemRequest = new PutItemRequest().
withTableName("Book").withItem(item);

// Call put item method from dynamodb client
PutItemResult putItemresult = dynamoDBClient.putItem(putItemRequest);
```

Get item

This method allows you to retrieve a stored item from a specified table identified by a specified primary key. The inputs required to be provided are table name and primary key. The following is the syntax for this:

```
//Create key instance for item to be fetched
HashMap<String, AttributeValue> key = new HashMap<String,
AttributeValue>();
    key.put("bookId", new AttributeValue().withN("2001"));

// Create get item request
```

```
GetItemRequest getItemRequest = new GetItemRequest().
withTableName("Book").withKey(key);

// Call getItem method from DynamoDB client
GetItemResult getItemResult = dynamoDBClient.getItem(getItemRequest);
```

You can also provide some additional attributes, such as attributes to fetch, consistency type (strong/eventual), and so on:

```
// List of attributes to be fetched
List<String> attributesTobeFetched = new ArrayList<String>(
    Arrays.asList("bookId", "name", "isbn", "authors"));

// Create key instance for item to be fetched
HashMap<String, AttributeValue> key = new HashMap<String,
AttributeValue>();
key.put("bookId", new AttributeValue().withN("2001"));

// Create get item request
GetItemRequest getItemRequest = new GetItemRequest()
      .withTableName("Book").withKey(key)
      .withAttributesToGet(attributesTobeFetched)
      .withConsistentRead(true);

// Call getItem method from DynamoDB client
GetItemResult getItemResult = dynamoDBClient.getItem(getItemRequest);
```

Update item

The update item method from DynamoDB client is quite a useful method that allows us to do multiple things in one go as follows:

- Modify existing value of an attribute
- Add a new attribute to an existing set
- Delete an attribute from an existing set

If you invoke the updateItem method for a non-existing item, then DynamoDB adds the new item to the table. You can also use the AttributeAction.ADD action to add a value to the existing set of values and do addition and subtraction for numeric values. The following is the syntax to use the updateItem method:

```
// Create Hash Map of item with attributes to be updated.
Map<String, AttributeValueUpdate> updateItems = new HashMap<String,
AttributeValueUpdate>();
```

```
// Add two new authors to the list.
updateItems.put("authors", new AttributeValueUpdate()
        .withAction(AttributeAction.ADD)
    .withValue(new AttributeValue().withSS("XYZ", "PQR")));

// Hash Map of key
HashMap<String, AttributeValue> primaryKey = new HashMap<String,
AttributeValue>();
primaryKey.put("bookId", new AttributeValue().withN("2001"));

// To increase the no. of chapters of the book by 2

updateItems.put("chapters", new AttributeValueUpdate()
    .withAction(AttributeAction.ADD)
    .withValue(new AttributeValue().withN("2")));

// To delete an attribute called "rating"
updateItems.put("rating", new AttributeValueUpdate()
        .withAction(AttributeAction.DELETE));

// finally create UpdateItemRequest and invoke updateItem method with
this request
UpdateItemRequest updateItemRequest = new UpdateItemRequest()
    .withKey(primaryKey)
    .withAttributeUpdates(updateItems);

UpdateItemResult updateItemResult = dynamoDBClient.
updateItem(updateItemRequest);
```

Delete item

Deleting an item from a table is quite easy; you can simply mention the primary key of the item to be deleted and the table name, as shown in the following code:

```
// Hash map of key
HashMap<String, AttributeValue> primaryKey = new HashMap<String,
AttributeValue>();
primaryKey.put("bookId", new AttributeValue().withN("2001"));

// Create delete item request with primary key and table name
DeleteItemRequest deleteItemRequest = new DeleteItemRequest()
.withKey(primaryKey)
```

```
.withTableName("Book");
// Invoke delete item method with prepared request
DeleteItemResult deleteItemResult = dynamoDBClient.
deleteItem(deleteItemRequest);
```

Batch get items

DynamoDB allows us to also get 100 items in one go. You can retrieve multiple items from multiple tables at a time. But, it is also important not to allow the size of the data retrieved to more than 1 MB, as shown in the following code:

```
// Create map of items to be fetched
HashMap<String, KeysAndAttributes> requestItems = new HashMap<String,
KeysAndAttributes>();

// Create list of keys to fetched
ArrayList<Map<String, AttributeValue>> keys = new
ArrayList<Map<String, AttributeValue>>();

// Key 1
HashMap<String, AttributeValue> key1 = new HashMap<String,
AttributeValue>();
    key1.put("bookId", new AttributeValue().withN("2001"));
    keys.add(key1);
// key 2
HashMap<String, AttributeValue> key2 = new HashMap<String,
AttributeValue>();
    key2.put("bookId", new AttributeValue().withN("2002"));
    keys.add(key2);

requestItems.put("Book", new KeysAndAttributes().withKeys(keys));

// Create Batch Get Item request
BatchGetItemRequest batchGetItemRequest = new BatchGetItemRequest().
withRequestItems(requestItems);

// invoke batch get items method
BatchGetItemResult batchGetItemResult = dynamoDBClient.batchGetItem(ba
tchGetItemRequest);
```

Batch write items

This API allows us to put or delete up to 25 items from multiple tables in one go, as shown in the following code:

```
// Create a map for the requests
Map<String, List<WriteRequest>> writeRequestItems = new
HashMap<String, List<WriteRequest>>();

// Create put request and add new book item in it

Map<String, AttributeValue> bookItem1 = new HashMap<String,
AttributeValue>();
    bookItem1.put("bookId", new AttributeValue().withS("2010"));
    bookItem1.put("name", new AttributeValue().withN("AWS EMR"));

Map<String, AttributeValue> bookItem2 = new HashMap<String,
AttributeValue>();
    bookItem2.put("bookId", new AttributeValue().withS("2011"));
    bookItem2.put("name", new AttributeValue().withN("AWS SWF"));

List<WriteRequest> bookList = new ArrayList<WriteRequest>();
    bookList.add(new WriteRequest().withPutRequest(new PutRequest().
withItem(bookItem1)));
    bookList.add(new WriteRequest().withPutRequest(new PutRequest().
withItem(bookItem2)));

writeRequestItems.put("Book", bookList);

// Create Put Batch Item request and invoke write batch write item
request

BatchWriteItemRequest batchWriteItemRequest = new BatchWriteItemReques
t(writeRequestItems);

BatchWriteItemResult batchWriteItemResult = dynamoDBClient.batchWriteI
tem(batchWriteItemRequest);
```

Using the AWS SDK for .NET

As we saw in table operations, a similar SDK is available in .NET as well.
The following are some examples to show how to perform item operations
using the .NET API:

Put item

To invoke the `putItem` method from DynamoDB client, we first need to create
a put item request, as shown in the following code:

```
var request = new PutItemRequest
{
    TableName = "Book",
    Item = new Dictionary<string, AttributeValue>()
        {
            { "bookId", new AttributeValue { N = "2001" }},
            { "name", new AttributeValue { S = "AWS DynamoDB" }},
            { "isbn", new AttributeValue { S = "2222-222-222" }},
            {
              "authors",
              new AttributeValue
              { SS = new List<string>{"XYZ", "PQR"}   }
            }
        }
};
dynamodbClient.PutItem(request);
```

Get item

To retrieve a particular item from a given table, you just need to simply mention its
key, as shown in the following code:

```
var request = new GetItemRequest
 {
    TableName = "Book",
    Key = new Dictionary<string,AttributeValue>() { { "bookId", new
AttributeValue { N = "2001" } } },
 };
 var response = dynamodbClient.GetItem(request);
```

Update item

The update item API allows us to add a new attribute to an existing set, delete an attribute from an existing set, or add a new attribute to an item. It can be done using the following code:

```
var request = new UpdateItemRequest
{
    TableName = "Book",
    Key = new Dictionary<string,AttributeValue>() { { "bookId", new
AttributeValue { N = "2001" } } },
    AttributeUpdates = new Dictionary<string, AttributeValueUpdate>()
    {
      // Add two new author to the list.
      { "authors",
        new AttributeValueUpdate
          {
              Action="ADD",
              Value = new AttributeValue{SS = { "XYZ", "PQR" }}
          }
      },
      // Increase the number of chapters by 2
      { "chapters",
        new AttributeValueUpdate
          {
              Action="ADD",
              Value = new AttributeValue{N = "2"}
          }
      },
      // Add a new attribute.
      { "pages",
        new AttributeValueUpdate  { Value = new AttributeValue{N =
"180" } } },

      // Delete the existing ISBN attribute.
      { "isbn", new AttributeValueUpdate  { Action="DELETE" } }
    }
};
var response = dynamodbClient.UpdateItem(request);
```

Delete item

You can delete an existing item from a particular table by specifying its primary key, as shown in the following code:

```
var request = new DeleteItemRequest
 {
    TableName = "Book",
```

```
    Key = new Dictionary<string,AttributeValue>() { { "bookId", new
AttributeValue { N = "2001" } } },
  };
var response = dynamodbClient.DeleteItem(request);
```

BatchGetItems

This API allows fetching of up to 100 items from multiple tables at a time. One thing to note is the request data size should not exceed the maximum limit of 1 MB. It can be used as shown in the following code:

```
string tableName = "Book";
var request = new BatchGetItemRequest
{
  RequestItems = new Dictionary<string, KeysAndAttributes>()
  {
    { tableName,
      new KeysAndAttributes
      {
        Keys = new List<Dictionary<string, AttributeValue>>()
        {
          new Dictionary<string, AttributeValue>()
          {
            { "bookId", new AttributeValue { N = "2010" } }
          }

          },
          new Dictionary<string, AttributeValue>()
          {
            { "bookId", new AttributeValue { N = "2011" } }

          }
        }
      }
    }
  }
};
var response = dynamodbClient.BatchGetItem(request);
```

BatchWriteItems

This API allows us to put and delete multiple items at a time. You need to create a proper batch write item request specifying what needs to be added and what needs be deleted.

In the following code, we are adding one item in the `Author` table and then deleting one item from the same table:

```
string tableName = "Author";
var request = new BatchWriteItemRequest
  {
      {
         tableName, new List<WriteRequest>
         {

           new WriteRequest
           {
             PutRequest = new PutRequest
             {
                Item = new Dictionary<string,AttributeValue>
                {
                   { "authId", new AttributeValue { N = "5001" } },
          { "name", new AttributeValue { S = "James Bond" } },
                   { "country", new AttributeValue { S = "USA" } },
                   { "topics", new AttributeValue { SS = new
  List<string> { "Hadoop", "Cloud" }  } }
                }
             }
           },
           new WriteRequest
           {
              DeleteRequest = new DeleteRequest
              {
                 Key = new Dictionary<string,AttributeValue>()
                 {
                    { "authId", new AttributeValue { N = "5002"  } }
                 }
              }
           }
         }
      }
   };
response = client.BatchWriteItem(request);
```

Using the AWS SDK for PHP

As we know AWS provides PHP APIs for table operations; we have the same for item operations as well.

The putItem method

To add an item to a DynamoDB table, we can use the `putItem` method. The following is an example of how to add a new book item to the `Book` table:

```
$response = $client->putItem(array(
    "TableName" => "Book",
    "Item" => array(
        "bookId"      => array( Type::NUMBER     => 2001),
        "name"     => array( Type::STRING      => "Dynamo DB" ),
        "isbn"     => array( Type::STRING      => "978-233435-555" ),
        "chapters"    => array( Type::NUMBER     => 10 ),
        "authors"  => array( Type::STRING_SET  => array("XYZ", "PQR")
    )
    )
));
```

The getItem method

We can retrieve the stored item in a DynamoDB table, as shown in the following code:

```
$response = $client->getItem(array(
    "TableName" => "Book",
    "Key" => array(
        "bookId" => array( Type::NUMBER => 2001 )
    )
));
```

The updateItem method

The `updateItem` API allows us to perform multiple operations, such as add a new attribute to an item, add an extra value to an existing set of attribute values, and delete an attribute from an existing item. It can be used as shown in the following code:

```
$response = $client->updateItem(array(
    "TableName" => "Book",
        "Key" => array(
            "bookId" => array(
                Type::NUMBER => 2001
            )
```

```
        ),
        "AttributeUpdates" => array(
            "authors" => array(
                "Action" => AttributeAction::PUT,
                "Value" => array(
                    Type::STRING_SET => array("XYZ", "PQR")
                )
            ),

            "chapters" => array(
                "Action" => AttributeAction::ADD,
                "Value" => array(
                    Type::NUMBER => 2
                )
            ),
            "pages" => array(
                "Action" => AttributeAction::DELETE
            )
        )
));
```

In the previous code snippet, we first added two extra authors in the `authors` attribute, increased the number of `chapters` by 2, and then deleted attribute `pages` from the item with `bookId` 2001.

The deleteItem method

Deleting an item is quite an easy job; you can simply invoke the `deleteItem` method specifying the table name and item primary key, as shown in the following code:

```
$response = $client->deleteItem(array(
    'TableName' => 'Book',
    'Key' => array(
        'Id' => array(
            Type::NUMBER => 2001
        )
    )
));
```

The batchGetItem API

With the `batchGetItem` API, we can fetch multiple items from various tables in one go. In the following code, we are fetching two items from the `Authors` table at a time.

```
$response = $client->batchGetItem(array(
    "RequestItems" => array(
```

```
            "Authors" => array(
                "Keys" => array(
                    array( // Key #1
                        "authId"  => array( Type::NUMBER => "5001"),

                    ),
                    array( // Key #2
                        "Id"  => array( Type::NUMBER => "5002"),
                    ),
                )
            )
    )));
```

The batchWriteItems API

The `batchWriteItems` API is a multiple purpose API that allows us to do things such as adding multiple items to multiple tables, deleting item/s from multiple tables, or adding an attribute to an existing item. Have a look at the following code:

```
$response = $client->batchWriteItem(array(
    "RequestItems" => array(
        "Book" => array(
            array(
                "PutRequest" => array(
                    "Item" => array(
                        "bookId"   => array(Type::NUMBER => 2020),
                        "name" => array(Type::STRING => "Mastering
Cassandra")
                    )
                )
            )
        ),
         "Author" => array(
            array(
                "PutRequest" => array(
                    "Item" => array(
                "authId"   => array(Type::NUMBER => 5001),
                        "name"   => array(Type::STRING => "Mark
Brown"),
                        "country" => array(Type::STRING => "UK"),
                        "topics"=>array(Type::STRING_SET =>
array("Hadoop", "Cloud"))
                    ))
                ),
                array(
```

```
                "DeleteRequest" => array(
                    "Key" => array(
                        "authId"   => array(Type::NUMBER => 5002)
                    ))
                )
            )
        )
    ));
```

In the previous example, we added an item to the `Book` table, added an item to the `Author` table, and deleted an item from the `Author` table.

Query and scan operations

The query operation is a very important operation that allows us to fetch specific items from the given table. It needs a primary input and an optional start key to compare with the list of items. The query fetches all matching entries to the input from a given table. You can also use comparison operations, such as greater than, less than, contains, between, and so on to narrow down the result set. Data returned from a query or scan operation is limited to 1 MB. If it does not find any matching items with respect to a given input key, it returns an empty set.

Query results are always sorted in the order of the range key value. By default, the order of sorting is ascending. If a table has secondary index, then the query operation can be performed on it as well.

The scan operation checks every individual item for a given table. We can specify the filter criteria in order to manage the search results after the scan gets completed. A scan filter normally consists of the list of attribute values to be compared with and the comparison operator. Like the query operator, the scan also puts the maximum result size as 1 MB.

Query versus scan

Even though the query and scan operations are meant to get bulk data depending on the given criteria, there are lots of fundamental differences between these operations. From a performance point of view, a query is much more efficient than the scan operation, as a query works on a limited set of items, while the scan operation churns the entire table data. The scan operation first returns the entire table data and then applies filters on it to remove the unnecessary data from the result set. So, it's obvious that as your table data grows, the scan operation would take more time to give back the results.

The query operation's performance is totally dependent on the amount of data retrieved. The number of matching keys for a given search criteria decides the query performance. If a specific hash key has more matching range keys than the size limit of 1 MB, then you can use pagination where an ExclusiveStartKey parameter allows you to continue your search from the last retrieved key by an earlier request. You need to submit a new query request for this.

Query results can be either eventually consistent or optionally strongly consistent, while scan results are eventually consistent only. The capacity unit calculation for query and scan is similar to other operations in DynamoDB, which we have already seen.

Pagination

As we discussed earlier, DynamoDB puts a size limit of 1 MB on the result set of query and scan operations. So, sometimes it's quite possible that the result set would have a dataset of more than 1 MB. In order to deal with this limitation, DynamoDB provides us with two useful parameters, LastEvaluatedKey and ExclusiveStartKey, which allow us to fetch results in pages. If a query or scan result reaches the maximum size limit of 1 MB, then you can put the next query by setting ExclusiveStartKey derived from LastEvaluatedKey. When DynamoDB reaches the end of search results, it puts LastEvaluatedKey as null.

Limit and counts

If you want to limit the number of results returned by the query and scan operations, then you can specify the limit parameter,which would limit the results to the specified number. Similar to the way we use limit from a RDBMS, this limit can also be used to do data sampling.

Like select count queries in a traditional RDBMS, we have something similar to that, which is also called count. If you set the count parameter to true in the query or scan request, then instead of returning the actual data set, DynamoDB returns the count of matching items for the given criteria. The data size limit of 1 MB is also applied for query and scan counts.

Parallel scan

DynamoDB's scan operation processes the data sequentially from the table, which means that, for a complete table scan, DynamoDB first retrieves 1 MB of data, returns it, and then goes and scans the next 1 MB of data, which is quite a nasty and time-consuming way of dealing with huge table scans.

Though Dynamo stores data on multiple logical partitions, a scan operation can only work on one partition at a time. This type of restriction leads to underutilization of the provisioned throughput.

To address all these issues, DynamoDB introduced the parallel scan, which divides the table into multiple segments, and multiple threads work on a single segment at a time. Here multiple threads and processes are invoked together, and each retrieve 1 MB of data every time. The process that works upon each segment is called a worker. To issue a parallel scan, you need to provide the `TotalSegments` value; `TotalSegments` is simply the number of workers going to access a certain table in parallel.

Suppose you have three workers, then you need to invoke the `scan` command in the following manner:

```
Scan (TotalSegments = 3, Segment = 0,..)
Scan (TotalSegments = 3, Segment = 1,..)
Scan (TotalSegments = 3, Segment = 2,..)
```

Here, we would logically divide the table into three segments, and each thread would scan a dedicated segment only. The following is the pictorial representation of a parallel scan:

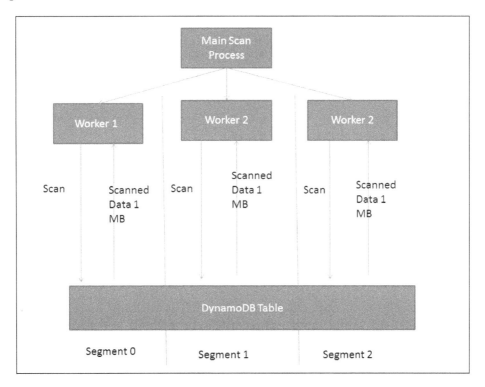

You can play around with `Segment` and `TotalSegments` values until you get the best performance for your scan request. The best use of the parallel scan is when we integrate DynamoDB with other AWS services, such as AWS EMR and AWS RedShift, as with this feature, the import/export from DynamoDB allows maximum utilization of provisioned resources.

Query and scan operations support a growing number of comparison operations; you can read more about them at `http://docs.aws.amazon.com/amazondynamodb/latest/APIReference/API_Condition.html`.

Querying tables

In this section, we are going to see how to programmatically query DynamoDB tables using Java, .NET, and PHP.

Using the AWS SDK for Java

To query DynamoDB data, you need to first create the DynamoDB client and invoke the query method from the same. The following code snippet shows how the Query API can be used to search `Book` with a given book ID:

```
// Create condition instance with hash key to searched
Condition condition = new Condition()
   .withComparisonOperator(ComparisonOperator.EQ)
   .withAttributeValueList(new AttributeValue().withN("2001"));

//create map of key conditions and add the condition

Map<String, Condition> conditions = new HashMap<String, Condition>();
   conditions.put("bookId", condition);

// Create query request

QueryRequest queryRequest = new QueryRequest().withTableName("Book").
withKeyConditions(conditions);

// Invoke query method from dynamodb client

QueryResult queryResult = dynamoDBClient.query(queryRequest);
```

You can also specify some optional parameters, such as attribute, to get, consistent read or eventual read, limit (number of records to be fetched), and so on.

For pagination, you can use `ExclusiveStartKey` and `LastEvaluatedKey` as explained earlier and shown in the following code:

```
Map<String, AttributeValue> lastEvaluatedKey = null;
    do {
        QueryRequest qryRequest = new QueryRequest()
                .withTableName("Book")
                .withKeyConditions(conditions)
                .withLimit(20)
                .withExclusiveStartKey(lastEvaluatedKey);
        QueryResult result = dynamoDBClient.query(qryRequest);
        for (Map<String, AttributeValue> resItem : result.getItems())
{
            System.out.println(resItem);
        }
        lastEvaluatedKey = result.getLastEvaluatedKey();
    } while (lastEvaluatedKey != null);
    }
```

The previous code snippet would fetch the book query results in 20 records per cycle.

Using the AWS SDK for .NET

Similar to Java, we need to create a query request in .NET and invoke a query method from the DynamoDB client using the following code:

```
var request = new QueryRequest
{
  TableName = "Book",
  KeyConditions = new Dictionary<string,Condition>()
  {
    {
      "yop",
      new Condition()
      {
        ComparisonOperator = "EQ",
        AttributeValueList = new List<AttributeValue>()
        {
          new AttributeValue { N = 2014 }
        }
      }
    }
  }
};

var response = dynamoDBClient.Query(request);
var result = response.QueryResult;
```

Here we are querying all books whose year of publishing (yop) is 2014 in the Book table.

If you want to see results in pages, the following is the syntax for it:

```
Dictionary<string,AttributeValue> lastKeyEvaluated = null;
do
{
  var request = new QueryRequest
  {
    TableName = "Book",
    KeyConditions = new Dictionary<string,Condition>()
    {
      {
        "yop",
        new Condition()
        {
          ComparisonOperator = "EQ",
          AttributeValueList = new List<AttributeValue>()
          {
            new AttributeValue { N = 2014 }
          }
        }
      }
    },
    // Setting page limit to 20
    Limit = 20,
    ExclusiveStartKey = lastKeyEvaluated
  };

  var response = dynamoDBclient.Query(request);
  // Printing query results
  foreach (Dictionary<string, AttributeValue> item in response.
QueryResult.Items)
  {
    PrintItem(item);
  }
  lastKeyEvaluated = response.QueryResult.LastEvaluatedKey;

} while (lastKeyEvaluated != null);
```

PHP API

The following is the syntax to query the Book table where the year of publishing equals 2014 in PHP:

```
$response = $client->query(array(
    "TableName" => "Book",
    "KeyConditions" => array(
        "yop" => array(
            "ComparisonOperator" => ComparisonOperator::EQ,
            "AttributeValueList" => array(
                array(Type::NUMBER => 2014)
            )
        )
    )
));
```

To use pagination, you can use the following code:

```
$tableName = "Book";
do {

    $request = array(
        "TableName" => $tableName,
        "KeyConditions" => array(
            "yop" => array(
                "ComparisonOperator" => ComparisonOperator::EQ,
                "AttributeValueList" => array(
                    array(Type::NUMBER => 2014)
                )
            )
        ),

        "Limit" => 20
    );

    # Add ExclusiveStartKey if it has got one in previous response
    if(isset($response) && isset($response['LastEvaluatedKey'])) {
        $request['ExclusiveStartKey'] = $response['LastEvaluatedKey'];
    }
    $response = $client->query($request);
} while(isset($response['LastEvaluatedKey']));
```

Scanning tables

In this section, we are going to see how to programmatically scan tables in different languages, such as Java, .NET, and PHP.

Using the AWS SDK for Java

To scan the table, you simply need to create the `scan` request and invoke the `scan` method from the DynamoDB client, specifying the table name, as shown in the following code:

```
// Create scan request
ScanRequest scanRequest = new ScanRequest().withTableName("Book");
// Invoke scan method
ScanResult  scanResult = dynamoDBClient.scan(scanRequest);
```

You can also specify an optional parameter, such as scan filter and attributes to get. You can read more about the scan filter and attributes to get at http://docs.aws.amazon.com/amazondynamodb/latest/APIReference/API_Scan.html.

For pagination, you need to write the code as follows:

```
Map<String, AttributeValue> lastKeyEvaluated = null;
do {
    ScanRequest scanRequest = new ScanRequest()
        .withTableName("Book")
        .withLimit(20)
        .withExclusiveStartKey(lastKeyEvaluated);

    ScanResult result = dynamoDBClient.scan(scanRequest);
    for (Map<String, AttributeValue> resItem: result.getItems()){
        System.out.println(resItem);
    }
    lastKeyEvaluated = result.getLastEvaluatedKey();
} while (lastKeyEvaluated != null);
```

Here we are scanning the `Book` table, 20 rows at a time.

Using the AWS SDK for .NET

To scan a table using a .NET API, you need to create the `scan` request and invoke the `scan` method by providing the details as shown in the following code:

```
var request = new ScanRequest
{
    TableName = "Book",
```

```
};

var response = dynamoDBClient.Scan(request);
var result = response.ScanResult;
```

You can also specify additional optional attributes, such as a scan filter and attributes to get. We can get the paginated results for the scan, as shown in the following code:

```
Dictionary<string, AttributeValue> lastKeyEvaluated = null;
do
{
    var request = new ScanRequest
    {
        TableName = "Book",
        Limit = 20,
        ExclusiveStartKey = lastKeyEvaluated
    };

    var response = dynamoDBClient.Scan(request);

    foreach (Dictionary<string, AttributeValue> item
      in response.Items)
    {
        PrintItem(item);
    }
    lastKeyEvaluated = response.LastEvaluatedKey;

} while (lastKeyEvaluated.Count != 0);
```

Using the AWS SDK for PHP

To scan a table in DynamoDB, you need to invoke the scan method from the DynamoDB client, as shown in the following code:

```
$response = $client->scan(array(
    "TableName" => "Book"
));
```

To use pagination, you need to write code in the following manner:

```
$tableName = "Book";

do {

    $request = array(
        "TableName" => $tableName,
```

```
            "Limit" => 20
        );

        # Add ExclusiveStartKey if present in previous response
        if(isset($response) && isset($response['LastEvaluatedKey'])) {
            $request['ExclusiveStartKey'] = $response['LastEvaluatedKey'];
        }

        $response = $client->scan($request);

    } while(isset($response['LastEvaluatedKey']));
```

Modeling relationships

Like any other database, modeling relationships is quite interesting even though DynamoDB is a NoSQL database. Now that we have learned about the DynamoDB's data model, we can start looking at how to use them in your application. Most of the time, people get confused on how to model the relationships between various tables. In this section, we are trying to make an effort to simplify this problem.

Let's try to understand the relationships better using our example of the bookstore, where we have entities, such as book, author, publisher, and so on.

One to one

In this type of relationship, a one-entity record of a table is related to only a one-entity record of the other table. In our bookstore application, we have the BookInfo and BookDetails tables. The BookInfo table can have information in brief about the book, which can be used to display book information on web pages, whereas the BookDetails table would be used when someone explicitly needs to see all the details of the book. This design helps us keep our system healthy as, even if there are a large number of requests on one table, the other table would always be up and running to fulfill what it is supposed to do. The following screenshot shows how the table structure would look:

Book Info Table	(Hash Key=bookId)
bookId=book1	{"title":"AWS EC2", "price": 30, "author":"ABC"}
bookId=book2	{"title":"AWS S3", "price": 40, "author":"XYZ"}

Book Details Table	(Hash Key=bookId)
bookId=book1	{"title":"AWS EC2" ,"isbn"":"111-111-111","pages":180, "price": 30, "author":"ABC"}
bookId=book2	{"title":"AWS S3" ,"isbn"":"111-111-2222","pages":200, "price": 40, "author":"XYZ"}}

One to many

In this type of relationship, one record from an entity is related to more than one record in another entity. In our bookstore application, we can have the `Publisher Book` table, which would keep information about the book and publisher relationship. Here, we can have `Publisher Id` as the hash key and `Book Id` as the range key. The following screenshot shows how a table structure would look:

Publisher Book Table		
Publisher Id (Hash Key)	Book Id (Range Key)	Attributes
publisherId=pub1	bookId=book1	{"yearOfPublication": 2014}
publisherId=pub2	bookId=book2	{"yearOfPublication": 2013}
publisherId=pub1	bookId=book3	{"yearOfPublication": 2013}

Many to many

A many-to-many relationship means many records from an entity are related to many records from another entity. In the case of our bookstore application, we can say that a book can be authored by multiple authors, and an author can write multiple books. In this we should use two tables with both hash and range keys, as shown in the following screenshot:

Book Table	Hash Key=bookId	Range Key=authId
bookId=book1	authId=alice	{"title":"AWS EC2" ,"isbn"":"111-111-111","pages":180}
bookId=book2	authId=bob	{"title":"AWS S3" ,"isbn"":"111-111-2222","pages":200}
bookId=book1	authId=cate	{"title":"AWS SWF" ,"isbn"":"111-111-3333","pages":200}

Author Table	Hash Key=authId	Range Key=bookId
authId=alice	bookId=book1	{ "age": 45, "country":"USA"}
authId=bob	bookId=book2	{"age": 35, "country":"INDIA"}
authId=cate	bookId=book1	{"age": 32, "country":"USA"}

In the previous screenshot, the Book table says that one book can have multiple authors, while the Author table says that an author can write multiple books.

Summary

In this chapter, we talked in detail about various aspects of the DynamoDB data model. We started with understanding the hash key, the range key, and their usage: secondary indexes, and how to use them in your application; and then we talked about various data types used in DynamoDB. We also discussed how to perform various operations on tables, items, and attributes using Java, .NET, and PHP APIs.

Now that we have learned how to use DynamoDB, it's time to understand how things work in the actual background. In the next chapter, we will discuss the architectural details of DynamoDB.

3
How DynamoDB Works

In the previous chapter, we saw the features DynamoDB has, and learned how to perform various operations on DynamoDB using a variety of APIs. We also saw various application-oriented examples, and what features of DynamoDB fit well in what conditions. Now it's time to understand its internals. In this chapter, we are going to talk about why DynamoDB was developed. What is the architecture underneath that makes it so robust and scalable? How does DynamoDB handle failures? So, let's get started.

In *Chapter 1*, *Getting Started*, we discussed DynamoDB's history; DynamoDB was built to address the scaling needs of Amazon's worldwide e-commerce platform, and also provide high availability, reliability, and performance. Amazon's platform is highly decoupled, consisting of thousands of services running on storage machines. Amazon needs reliable storage systems that can store and retrieve data even in conditions like disk failures, network failures, or even during natural calamities, which means that a user should be able to add/remove items in/from the cart, make payments, and do checkouts 24*7 without any downtime, as even a few minutes of downtime may have major financial implications. When you have many decoupled components, it is expected to have machine and network failures, so DynamoDB was designed in such a manner that it handles failures as a normal case and should not affect the performance and availability of the system.

DynamoDB uses a combination of the best-known techniques, which, combined together have formed such a brilliant system. It uses a consistent hashing algorithm to achieve uniform data partitioning. Object versioning is done for consistency. The quorum technique is used to maintain consistency amongst the replicas. Now, let's try to dive deep into more such techniques and try to understand what role these techniques play in DynamoDB's system architecture.

Service-oriented architecture

Amazon's platform is fully service oriented, which means various components in Amazon's ecosystem are exposed as a service for the other services to consume. Each service has to maintain its SLA in order to complete the response accurately and on time. SLA is a Service Level Agreement where a service agrees to provide a response within the said time for a said number of requests per second. In Amazon's service-oriented architecture, it is very important for services to maintain the agreement, as Amazon's request response engine builds the response dynamically by combining the results from many services. Even to answer a single request on Amazon's e-commerce website, hundreds of services come together to form the response.

In the following diagram, the request comes from the web via Amazon's e-commerce platform, which is then forwarded to various services to get the appropriate data from DynamoDB. Data transfer happens in DynamoDB from simple APIs like GET/PUT/DELETE. The data from various services gets aggregated, and then it's provided to the page rendering service, which actually builds the page.

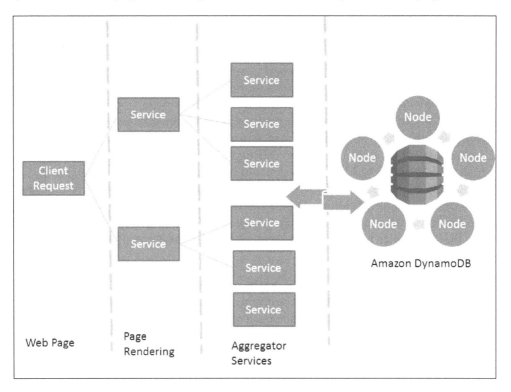

Also, as you see in the diagram, DynamoDB does not have any master node or superior node that would control everything. Rather, it maintains a ring structure of nodes, where each node would have equal responsibilities to perform.

Design features

While deciding DynamoDB's architecture, several design considerations have been made that were quite new at that time, and over time these techniques have become so popular that it has inspired many NoSQL databases we are using these days. The following are a few such features:

- Data replication
- Conflict resolution
- Scalability
- Symmetry
- Flexibility

Data replication

While deciding upon the data replication strategy, Amazon engineers put significant focus on achieving high availability and reliability. Traditional data replication techniques used to have synchronous replica update, which means that if the value for a certain attribute gets changed, it would be updated with all its replicas at that point of time only, and unless that is done, access to that attribute would be made unavailable. This technique was used in order to avoid wrong or stale data being provided to the user. But this technique was not that efficient, as networks and disks are bound to fail and waiting for all data replicas to get updates was really time consuming.

So, to avoid this, engineers decided to stick with eventual consistency, which means that replicas would be updated asynchronously by a background process. This solution solved the problem of availability but gave rise to one more problem, that is, conflicts. If a node gets updated with a new attribute value, an asynchronous process will start updating the replicas in the background. Suppose, that one of the nodes where a replica for the same data resides is not available for update, then that node would have the same old value. Meanwhile, if the node becomes available again and gets a read request, then it would present the old value, and there would be a conflict between this node and other nodes.

Conflict resolution

Earlier, we saw that eventual consistency in data replication leads to conflicts, so it's very important to handle the conflict resolution in a neat and clean manner. For conflict resolution, we need to answer two things:

- When to resolve the conflict?
- Who would be resolving the conflict?

Conflicts can be resolved at read time or write time. Most data store systems resolve conflicts on write operations and keep the read operation fast and lightweight. But DynamoDB does not do that; it uses an always writable strategy, allowing writes all the time. This is a crucial strategy from Amazon's business point of view, as they don't want people to wait for some write to happen until the conflict is resolved. This means they want the user to be able to add items to the cart at all times. If it does not happen, then it would give a bad user experience and would lead to a serious impact on Amazon's business.

It is also equally important to decide who would resolve the conflict, that is, the application or the database. When it comes to the database resolving conflicts, it prefers to use the *last write wins* strategy. In the case of Amazon, you are given the choice to choose your own conflict resolution by providing features such as conditional writes, which we saw in *Chapter 2*, *Data Models*.

Scalability

The most important design consideration was to have a system that can be scaled out easily without affecting the application. DynamoDB uses the ring topology to arrange its nodes. So, whenever there is a need to scale up the cluster, you can easily add a node to the existing cluster without affecting system performance. Make a note that as a DynamoDB service user, we don't have access to scale up or scale down clusters; what we can do for this is to increase or decrease the provisioned throughput.

Symmetry

DynamoDB targets symmetry in its node cluster, which means that no node is the master node, neither do they perform extra work or have extra responsibility than others. This helps in maintaining the system properly balanced; plus, there is no need to worry about failures, as even if a node or two fails, the system would remain intact. There is no single point of failure in DynamoDB because of this.

Flexibility

DynamoDB's ring architecture allows nodes of different configurations to be a part of the same cluster, and each node gets the amount of responsibility it deserves. This gives us the flexibility to add nodes as and when they are required and of whatever size and configurations they are, they would be loaded with work.

Architecture

DynamoDB's architecture consists of various well-known, and a few new, techniques that have helped engineers build such a great system. To build a robust system like this, one has to consider various things, such as load balancing, partitioning, failure detection/prevention/recovery, replica management and their sync, and so on. In this section, we are going to focus on all these things, and learn about them in detail.

Load balancing

DynamoDB, being a distributed system, needs its data to be balanced across various nodes. It uses **consistent hashing** for distributing data across the nodes. Consistent hashing dynamically partitions the data over the network and keeps the system balanced.

Consistent hashing is a classic solution to a very complex problem. The secret is finding a node in a distributed cluster to store and retrieve a value identified by a key, while at the same time being able to handle the node failures. You would say this is quite easy, as you can simply number the servers and use some modulo hash function to distribute the load. But the real problem is not only finding the node for storage or retrieval but handling requests if a certain node goes down or is unreachable. At this point, you would be left with only one option, that is, to rearrange your hash numbering and rebalance the data. But doing this on each failure is a quite an expensive operation.

Consistent hashing uses a unique technique to solve this problem; here, both the nodes and the keys are hashed and the same technique is used for their lookup. We first create a hash space or hash ring. Determining a hash value for each node in a cluster is as good as placing that node on the circumference of the hash ring, as shown in the following diagram:

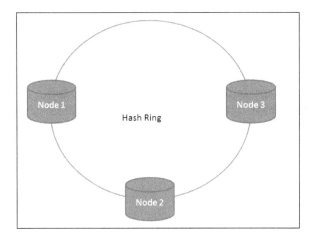

When a value associated with a key needs to be retrieved, first we calculate the hash of the key, which again corresponds to a place on the circle. In order to place or retrieve a key, one simply moves around the circle in a clockwise direction unless the next node is found. If no node is found in the given hash space, the first node is considered the place to store in, or retrieve from, as shown in the following diagram:

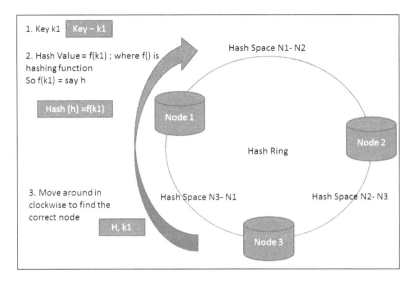

This way, each node becomes responsible for taking care of keys between itself and its previous node. This implementation of consistent hashing leads to a few issues: first, it may lead to uneven distribution of load as, if a key is not able to find a position, it will always go to the first node; second, it will also increase the difference in the performance of various nodes impacting the overall system. To address the issue of uneven load, DynamoDB uses a variant of consistent hashing, where it assigns a node to multiple points on the hash ring circle instead of on a single point as we saw in the basic algorithm earlier. DynamoDB puts multiple virtual nodes on the ring, which would represent a single physical machine. Doing so helps in making distribution of data even across the cluster.

In the case of node failure, the load managed by this node gets evenly distributed among the other nodes from the cluster, and if a new node gets introduced, then that node takes approximately an equal part of the load from the other nodes.

Data replication

Data replication in DynamoDB is handled by a special type of node called a **coordinator node**. The replication factor (N) is configured per instance, which is nothing but the number of replications of a certain key. The coordinator node first keeps the key on the local machine and then replicates it to N minus 1 successor machine in the clockwise direction, as shown in the following diagram:

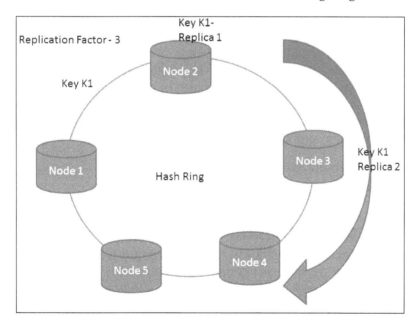

The previous diagram says that if you have a key, say, K1, which falls in the range Node1-Node2, then replicas of the key would be stored on two successor nodes of Node1. The list of nodes saving a particular key is called a preference list. While creating this list, we need to make sure that we don't have any virtual nodes, as they might be referencing the same node.

Data versioning and reconciliation

We know that DynamoDB is eventually consistent and it is write always, which means that all data object updates need to go through all replicas asynchronously. In order to avoid any data loss, DynamoDB keeps versions of objects. Later, these various versions get reconciled to give a uniform response. To maintain this, DynamoDB creates new, immutable objects for new updates, which means a certain object can have multiple versions of it in a DynamoDB system.

DynamoDB uses **vector clocks** to do the object versions and their conflict resolution. A vector clock is a mechanism that helps in maintaining various versions of an object and in resolving the conflicts. Let's understand the vector clock with an example. Suppose we have two nodes say, N1 and N2, then for a particular object vector clock with [0,0], the first zero stands for the object version on node N1 while the second 0 stands for the object version on node N2. Now, node N1 writes to the object and updates its vector clock as [1,0]. If the same thing happens with node N2, then it updates the vector clock as [0,1]. Meanwhile, if due to some network issues, these two nodes go out of sync, then they would not be able to understand each other's writes. This way, the conflicts are identified.

To resolve the conflicts, every data object keeps a context. If the same context is still present at the time of the write, there is no harm in more writes, and you can proceed further. In case of any conflict, we need to reconcile the data versions in order to maintain the exact value for a given key. DynamoDB uses various reconciliation strategies to resolve the conflicts:

- Logic-based reconciliation
- Time-based reconciliation

Logic-based reconciliation

In this method of reconciliation, the client who has requested the data object itself decides whether it has got the exact version of the data object it was looking for. Amazon's shopping cart service is a good example of logic-based reconciliation; here, in the event of any conflict, the business logic itself reconciles the object and solves the conflict.

Time-based reconciliation

This is the simplest algorithm used for reconciliation of different versions of data objects in DynamoDB. Here, the object version with the latest timestamp is supposed to be updated and used to return to the client. Here, we only need to make sure that the systems that have the replicas have their calendars in sync.

Request handling

The `get` and `put` requests in DynamoDB are handled in two ways: first, it can route through a load balancer, or it can directly select a node using partitioning information. In the first case, the load balancer decides which way the request would be routed, while in the second strategy, the client selects the node to contact. Both strategies are beneficial in their own ways; in the first strategy, the client is unaware of DynamoDB, which is helpful in terms of scalability and makes your architecture loosely coupled. The second strategy helps in achieving lower latency. As a DynamoDB user, we don't have any control over request handling, partitioning, or any other internals.

When a client sends a request to DynamoDB, it can be handled by any node in that cluster. When a node receives the request, it first checks whether that node has the given range of keys provided by the client. If it has got the key, it will fulfill the request, or else it will simply forward the request to the top N nodes in the preferred list.

Read and write operations involve only the top N healthy nodes. The nodes which are not available, or not reachable, are completely ignored. To maintain the consistency in replicas, DynamoDB uses a quorum-like technique to decide whether an operation should be declared successful or not in a distributed environment.

In quorum, we have to maintain two keys R (Read) and W (Write); here R is the minimum number of nodes that should participate in a successful read operation and W is the minimum number of nodes that should participate in a successful write operation. Here, we are expected to set R and W such that R plus W is greater than N, where N is the number of nodes in the cluster. This ensures the commits are done only in quorum, but there is one disadvantage of this technique, that this may lead to a lower response time as the latency would be decided by the slowest node. In order to avoid this, DynamoDB keeps the R plus W number less than N to get better latency.

When a coordinator node receives the `put()` request, it first generates a new version of the object in the vector clock and writes the update locally. The coordinator node then sends the update along with the updated vector clock to the N most reachable nodes. If at least W minus 1 nodes respond, then the write is supposed to be a successful one.

In the case of the `get()` operation, the coordinator node requests all available versions of data from the N most reachable nodes. If the coordinator node receives multiple versions of objects, then the responses are reconciled looking at the vector clock. Once done, the reconciled version of the object is returned to the client. Also, the same reconciled version is written to nodes that do not have the updated version of the data item. You can read more about quorum at `http://en.wikipedia.org/wiki/Quorum`.

Handling failures

There can be multiple reasons for failures in a distributed system, such as node failures, disk failures, network issues, power failures, or even natural or unnatural disasters. Data loss at any given cost is simply not acceptable. DynamoDB has various techniques to handle failures of the following types:

- Temporary failures
- Permanent failures

For temporary node failures, DynamoDB does not implement quorum-like techniques to determine the read and write consistency, as it has to consider the network and node failures. To achieve this, DynamoDB does not enforce strict quorum techniques; instead, it uses the sloppy quorum technique, which allows commits on a successful vote from the first N healthiest nodes of a cluster.

If a node fails, then the replica that needs to reside on the failed node gets persisted to some other available node. DynamoDB keeps metadata of all such data entries, and that table gets scanned frequently. This is done to maintain the durability and availability promise. The replica that was copied to some other node will carry a hint that gives information about the node where it was intended to get replicated. Once the failed node is back, the replica is restored on that node and the metadata is updated. This strategy is called **hinted handoff**.

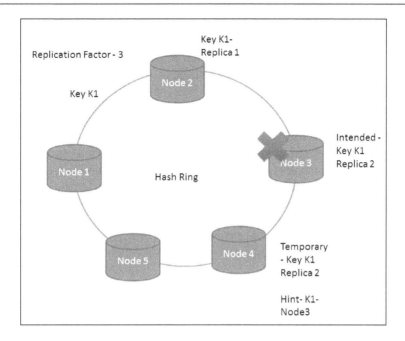

In the previous diagram, a replica of k1 was intended to be stored on Node 3, but at the time of storage, the node becomes unreachable. In that case, the replica gets stored on Node 4 with a hint saying that this piece of data originally belonged to Node 3. Once Node 3 becomes accessible again, the replica is placed back on that node.

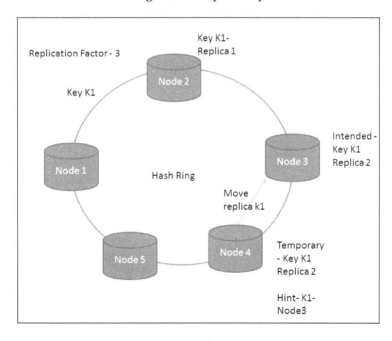

The hinted handoff works well if the number of nodes in a cluster is limited. Also, it might be the case that before the hinted replicas are replaced to the original intended node, the temporary node fails to handle such permanent failures. DynamoDB uses a very interesting replica synchronization technique for better results.

DynamoDB uses **Merkle tree** to maintain the replica synchronization. Comparing all existing replicas and updating replicas with the latest changes is called **AntiEntropy**. A Merkle tree is an algorithm used to store and compare objects. In a Merkle tree, the root node contains the hash of all children, and if the hash values of the root nodes of two trees are the same, then it means those two trees are equal. In the case of DynamoDB, we create a Merkle tree of the replica on each node and compare them. If the root hashes of trees are the same, then it means the replicas are in sync, whereas if the root hash is not the same, then that means that the replicas are out of sync, and then you can compare the next child nodes and find out the actual discrepancy.

Each DynamoDB node maintains a Merkle tree for each and every key range it has. Doing this, it allows DynamoDB to check whether certain key ranges are in sync or not. If it finds any discrepancy, then child-wise traversal is done to find the cause of the discrepancy, as shown in the following diagram:

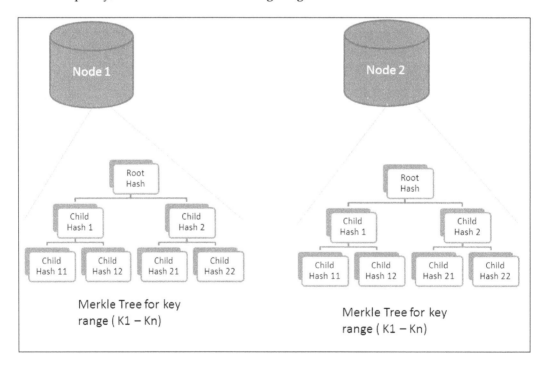

The preceding diagram shows how two nodes in a DynamoDB cluster form Merkle trees and compare hashes. This technique of replica synchronization is the same in Cassandra and Riak as well. You can read more about Merkle trees at `http://en.wikipedia.org/wiki/Merkle_tree`.

Ring membership

We have been talking about the ring membership of DynamoDB since the start. There might be a number of reasons to add or remove nodes from a DynamoDB cluster, such as storage outage, power /network disk failure, and so on. Some node failures might be temporary and need not require load balancing, as it can be time consuming and unnecessary. This is because after some time the node would be back. Similarly, someone can accidentally trigger a new node that might be taken off in minutes. So, it would be time consuming to do load balancing for all such accidental and temporary membership changes.

Keeping this in mind, DynamoDB relies on the administrator to initiate a membership change request and inform any one member in the DynamoDB cluster. The administrator is provided with a command line and browser tool to perform node addition or deletion. The node to whom the administrator initiates the membership change request writes the changes to other member nodes. A history is maintained to keep track of all membership change requests. DynamoDB uses a gossip-based protocol to propagate the changes made to its membership. Gossip protocol is a computer-to-computer communication style, where one computer initiates a communication with some computers, and then these computers forward the message to other computers, and so on. You can read more about gossip protocol at `http://en.wikipedia.org/wiki/Gossip_protocol`.

For the new node joining the cluster, it has to first choose the range of tokens on the hash ring. It also needs to have virtual nodes placed at various logical points on the hash ring. Once the node joins the ring, it has to take information from all the other nodes and the range of tokens/keys they handle, and vice versa. Each node needs to be aware of the token ranges handled by its peers in order to forward the requests to appropriate nodes.

The following diagram pictorially represents how membership changes are propagated to all nodes in a DynamoDB cluster:

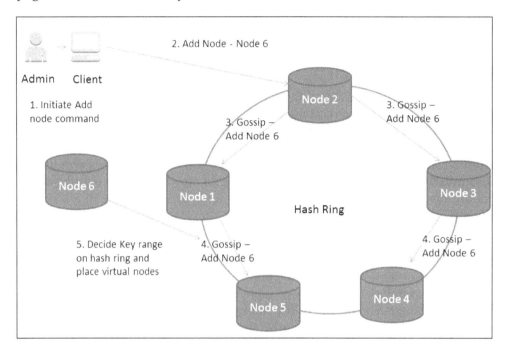

Seed nodes

It might be the case where the administrator adds two different nodes at a time, and during gossip, none of them would have information about each other. Also, there might be cases where DynamoDB would be partitioned into logical parts. To avoid such issues, DynamoDB keeps seed nodes that would have static information about the cluster. Some nodes from the cluster play the role of seed nodes. Seed nodes have all the information about the membership, as the information is derived from an external service. All nodes ultimately reconcile the membership information with seed nodes, and this helps in solving the previously mentioned problems.

Functional components

Till now, we have seen how DynamoDB's architecture provides so many features in terms of scalability, fault tolerance, availability, and so on. We also saw how ring membership is maintained and how it helps DynamoDB's desired specialities.

Each DynamoDB node consists of the following components:

- Request coordinator
- Membership and failure detection
- Local persistent store (storage engine)

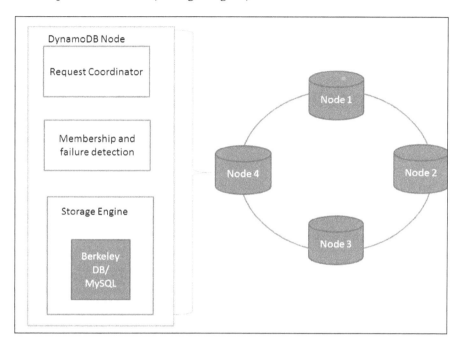

Request coordinator

The request coordinator is an event-driven messaging component that works like **Staged-Even Drive Architecture (SEDA)**. Here, we break the complex event into multiple stages. This decouples event and thread scheduling from application logic. You can read more about SEDA at www.eecs.harvard.edu/~mdw/proj/seda/. This component is mainly responsible for handling any client requests coming its way.

Suppose a coordinator receives a get request, then it asks for the data from the respective nodes where the key range lies. It waits till it gets the acceptable number of responses and does the reconciliation if required. If it receives a number of responses that is less than desired, then it fails the request. After the request is fulfilled, this process waits for some time if any delayed responses arrive. If any node returns stale data versions, then the coordinator updates data with the correct version on that node.

In the case of write requests, the top N nodes in the preferred list are chosen to store the update. It might be the case that a particular node appears in many preferred lists. Then, it would lead to uneven distribution of load. In that case, DynamoDB has an intelligent way to choose the write coordinator. Normally, it is seen that a write operation follows a read operation. So, the coordinator that has responded fastest in the previous read request is chosen to be the coordinator for the write operation. The information about the previous read operation can be obtained from context. This strategy is also useful in another way in that it writes the same data version that was read earlier.

Membership failure and detection

This component is responsible for maintaining the membership information of the node for a certain cluster. It also keeps track of any new node addition or removal and manages the key range accordingly.

All membership-related information, such as key hash ranges of peers and seed nodes, is maintained by this service. This is a very crucial component from the distributed system coordination point of view. We have already seen the details of ring membership and failure handling in previous sections.

Local persistence store

DynamoDB's local persistence store is a pluggable system where you can select the storage depending upon the application use. Generally, DynamoDB uses Berkeley DB or MySQL as the local persistence store. Berkeley DB is a high-performance embedded database library used for key-value pair type of storage. The storage is selected depending upon the application object size. Berkeley DB is used where object size has a maximum limit of 10 KB, while MySQL is used for application object size expected to be on the higher side.

Most of Amazon's production systems use Berkeley DB as their local storage. As an AWS customer, we don't have the choice to select our local persistence store though.

Berkeley DB is a library that is used as embedded data storage. It is written in C language and provides APIs to various languages, such as Java, C++, PHP, C#, and so on. It stores data in the key value format. The initial version of Berkeley DB was out way back in 1994; since then, it has seen many changes and upgrades. Currently, it is in development at Oracle Corporation.

Berkeley DB has three products under one umbrella, which are as follows:

- Berkeley DB, which is a traditional library written in C
- Berkeley DB Java Edition, which supports important Java features, such as POJOs, Collections, and so on
- Berkeley DB XML edition, which supports data storage of XML documents

Berkley DB provides local storage, underlying storage and retrieval for many databases, LDAP servers like MySQL, Oracle NoSQL, Subversion (SVN), MemcacheDB, RPM, and many more.

Summary

In this chapter, we have seen the design specifications of DynamoDB, various techniques like a quorum approach, gossip protocols, ring membership, and Merkle trees, and their implementation and benefits in developing such a brilliant system. We can see the efforts put in by the Amazon engineering team and their focus on each and every minute detail of architecture and its execution.

As I had said earlier, DynamoDB was the real inspiration for many NoSQL databases, such as Riak and Cassandra. Now, that you have understood the architectural details of DynamoDB, you can check out the architecture of previously mentioned databases and see the similarities and differences.

This chapter was an effort to simplify the information given by Amazon in its white paper, but as time flies, there would have been many changes in its architecture, and to know more about it, we would have to wait to hear it from Amazon.

I am sure if you are a real technology fan, then after reading this chapter, you would have definitely fallen in love with DynamoDB. In the next chapter, we are going to talk about the best practices one should follow in order to get the maximum benefit out of DynamoDB and save some money too.

4
Best Practices

When it comes to public cloud, most of the time each operation means money, be it a read operation or a write. Each operation gets counted in terms of capacity units or in terms of the number of calls made to the database. So while working on cloud, we have to be extremely careful about the usage, and we also need to make sure that the bills are constant and do not end up as a surprise to any organization.

Until now, we have seen various features of DynamoDB, its internals and how they work, and how to add/delete/update data to and from DynamoDB. Now that you have learned most of the details from DynamoDB's usage point view, it's time to learn some best practices one should follow in order to make the most of DynamoDB. I am sure the best practices we are going to cover in this chapter would certainly help in saving some bucks for you and your organization.

In this chapter, we will cover the following topics:

- Table-level best practices
- Item-level best practices
- Index-level best practices
- Efficient use of query and scan operations
- How to avoid sudden bursts of data

We will also be talking about various common use cases that can be used across multiple applications, save time and money, and help efficiency. Now let's start discussing the best practices one by one.

Table level best practices

We have already seen what a table means and how it used. There are various techniques with which we can maximize the table read/write efficiency.

Choosing a primary key

We have seen the primary key representations of DynamoDB, that is, the hash key and composite hash and range key. The hash key value decides how the items would get distributed across multiple nodes and the level parallelism. It's quite possible that some of the items in a table would be used heavily compared to others. In that case, one particular partition would be used frequently, and the rest of the partitions would range from unused to less-used, which is a bad thing considering the performance and throughput of the system. Now let's discuss some best practices in choosing the right hash key and composite hash and range key.

It is recommended that you should design your tables such that hash key of the table would be having the variety of data. It does not mean that your application must access all hash keys all the time, it means even if your application accesses multiple hash keys together, all such requests would get distributed across the cluster and there would not be any load on one particular node. Consider the following table which talks about hash keys, scenarios, and efficiency.

Table	Hash key	Scenario	Efficiency
Book	Book ID	Each book has a unique book ID, and there are a variety of books in a table	Good
Country	Country name	Limited number of countries	Bad
Songs	Song ID	Each song has a unique song ID, but one particular song is much more popular than others	Bad

The first scenario is the ideal scenario and has got the perfect choice hash key. This ensures that the load in the book table would be distributed across various nodes, which would result in a high degree of parallelism. The second scenario would be having some issues in terms of access as there are very few countries, and all the data would get gathered in only a few nodes. This would result in bad efficiency as the cluster would not be fully utilized, and this would result in high load on a few nodes and less or no load on others.

In the third scenario we have the songs table, which would contain multiple songs with each song having a unique song ID. But there is a big chance that one or two songs turn out to be more popular than any other song. This would also result in uneven use of the DynamoDB cluster.

To avoid creating hot partitions in DynamoDB, it is recommended to append a random number to the hash key. In our example, we saw that the songs table had a few songs that which were accessed more than others. In order to avoid creating a hot partition, we can append a random number to the most popular song IDs and save it as a completely new hash key. Suppose we have a song with the song ID 123, then it is recommended that we append random number between certain ranges and distribute the load so that we can have multiple items, such as 123-0, 123-1, 123-2, and so on.

This technique holds good to balance the write load. But when it comes to reading the data, you might get confused about which item to retrieve. So, to cater to this, you can decide upon a random number strategy based on the data available. For example, you can calculate the random number to be appended to a song ID based on the hash calculation of the song's name or the singer's name in such a way that when you want to retrieve that item, you can recalculate the number to be appended and search with that hash key.

One thing we have to make note of is that by doing this, we are creating multiple copies of the same data, and so if you are going to use it, you should also consider the efforts required to maintain these copies in sync.

Evenly distributed data upload

Sometimes, there is a need to upload data from different sources. At that time, uploading data in a distributed manner is a tedious task. Sometimes, we have both hash and range keys for certain tables. Consider an example of the tweets table where you would need to manage usernames and their respective tweets. In that case, you can have the username as the hash key and the tweet ID as the range key and upload the data in the following manner:

UserName	TweetID
User1	T1
User1	T2
User1	T3
User2	T1

UserName	TweetID
User2	T2
User3	T1
User3	T2

Here, if you request to get all messages from a particular user, then that request might not distribute the load evenly across the nodes. As you can see from the table, the first few requests would only be writing on the User1 partition, the next few would be writing on the User2 partition. While the writes are happening on the User1 partition, other partitions would be at rest, and all loads would only be on the User1 partition, which is definitely not a good sign from the distributed environment point of view.

A better way to design the same data upload would be to have one tweet per user and then repeat the same pattern again. This would perform a write request first on the User1 partition; the second one would be on the User2 partition, and so on. The following table shows the required sequence of data write requests:

UserName	TweetID
User1	T1
User2	T1
User3	T1
User1	T2
User2	T2
User3	T2
User1	T3

This would keep each and every node of the DynamoDB cluster busy and active, ultimately resulting in maximum utilization of resources and provisioned throughput.

In traditional database systems, it is beneficial to make your writes as sequential as possible as it would optimize the performance. But in the case of DynamoDB, we don't need to do that; rather, if we do so, we would end up underutilizing the provisioned throughput for the given table. So it is advised to shred your load to achieve high performance.

Managing time series data

Many times we have a requirement to store time series data in our database. We might be saving data in that table over years and the table size would keep growing. Consider the example of an order table where you would be saving orders made my customers. You can choose the order ID as the hash key and the date/time as the range. This strategy would certainly segregate the data, and you would be able to query data on order ID with date/time easily, but there is a problem with this approach as here there is a good chance recent data will be accessed more frequently than older data.

So, here we might end up creating some partitions as hot partitions, while others would be cold partitions. To solve this problem, it is recommended to create tables based on time range, which means creating a new table for each week or month instead of saving all data in the table. This strategy helps avoid the creation of any hot or cold partitions. You can simply query data for a particular time range table itself. This strategy also helps when you need to purge data where you can simply drop the tables you don't wish to see any more. Alternatively, you can simply dump that data on AWS S3, as flat files, which is a cheap data storage service from Amazon.

We are going to see how to integrate AWS S3 with DynamoDB in *Chapter 6, Integrating DynamoDB with Other AWS Components*.

Item best practices

There can be various ways in which we can improve item access, some of which we are going to discuss in this section.

Caching

Sometimes, we might need to use a certain item or set of items more frequently than others. Also, there is a good chance that lesser value updates will be made for such items. In this case, you can use caching to store items at cache level, and whenever required, you can simply fetch that from cache. The use of cache reduces the number of calls made to DynamoDB, hence improving the time and cost efficiency.

For example, you have a lookup table whose values are fixed and do not change over time, and there are a few items in that table that are very popular. In that case, you can simply use caching to store these items. For the very first time, when cache is blank, we would be fetching the data from the actual table itself.

The next time onwards, the program should check if the entry is present for the item in cache. If yes, then directly use that value; if not, then and then only get data from DynamoDB and update cache.

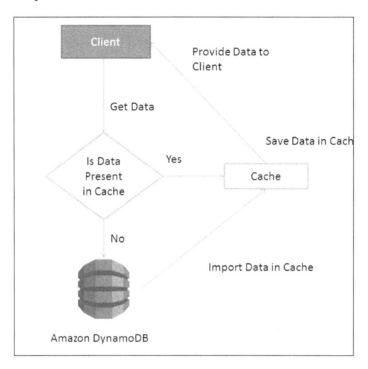

The previous diagram shows how caching works when a client tries to retrieve some information from DynamoDB. First, it checks if the required information is present in cache. If the information is present, then it simply returns the data to the client. But if the information is not present, then the program first fetches the data from DynamoDB, stores it in cache, and then returns the data to the client.

There are various types of caching techniques available, such as standalone, distributed, and so on. Depending upon the needs of your application, you can choose the best fit. For example, if you want to store a small set of data, then you can use in-memory cache libraries such as Ehcache, but if your caching needs are bigger, then you can use distributed cache such as Memcache, Oracle Coherence, and so on. Amazon also provides its own hosted caching as a service called ElasticCache. The choice is yours.

Storing large attribute values

We know that currently DynamoDB puts size constraints on each item that we put or retrieve. Also, each and every call to DynamoDB is money for us. So, in order to reduce the data size and ultimately the cost, we have various ways to deal with large attributes. Here are a few such techniques.

Using compressions

In *Chapter 2*, *Data Models*, we saw the data model of DynamoDB, where we covered various DynamoDB data types. We also saw what the binary data type is and how it is used. When we declare the data type of a certain attribute as binary, we would expect a huge attribute to get stored in it. So, in such cases, it is recommended that we compress such a binary attribute using well-known compression algorithms, such as gzip, LZO, and so on.

So, when we are going to store an item, we encode it using a certain algorithm that would reduce its length and size, and while retrieving that value, we decode it using a similar algorithm to get the original value back. This technique helps us to reduce the size of the data stored and retrieved, ultimately reducing the cost.

But one thing we should keep in mind is that even though using these algorithms would save storage space and money, it would also increase CPU time as we might need to invest some time in encoding and decoding the data. So, if you are comfortable with a slight delay in your data retrievals, then you must go and implement this technique and save some bucks for you and your organization.

The following is a sample Java code that you can use to compress a long string into gzip:

```java
public String compress(String inputString) throws IOException {
        if (inputString == null || inputString.length() == 0) {
            return inputString;
        }
        ByteArrayOutputStream out = new ByteArrayOutputStream();
        GZIPOutputStream gzip = new GZIPOutputStream(out);
        gzip.write(inputString.getBytes());
        gzip.close();
        String compressedStr = out.toString("ISO-8859-1");
        return compressedStr;
}
```

The previous function accepts the input string to be compressed and returns compressed gzip. Similarly, the decompress function accepts the compressed string, which returns the clear text original string back. Note that it is very important to use the same encoding while compressing and decompressing.

```
public static  String decompress(String inputString) throws
IOException {
        if (inputString == null || inputString.length() == 0) {
            return inputString;
        }
GZIPInputStream gis = new GZIPInputStream(new ByteArrayInputStream(inp
utString.getBytes("ISO-8859-1")));
BufferedReader bf = new BufferedReader(new InputStreamReader(gis,
"ISO-8859-1"));
String decompressedString = "";
String line;
        while ((line=bf.readLine())!=null) {
            decompressedString += line;
        }
        return decompressedString;

    }
```

Using AWS S3

As we discussed the size constraints put by Amazon on items, it is very important to have a solid solution to solve the issue of large items. One good solution is to store large attributes in AWS S3 buckets. Here, we can simply store the item in an AWS S3 bucket and have its object identifier stored in an item attribute. Here is an example to illustrate this. Suppose we want to store information about one research paper in a particular journal, which also contains some images. Now, it's obvious that images would have larger size compared to text. So, here we can store other text information about the paper in DynamoDB and store the images on AWS S3. To link the images and the item in DynamoDB, we can simply store the object identifier of the image as a metadata attribute in a DynamoDB item as shown in the following diagram:

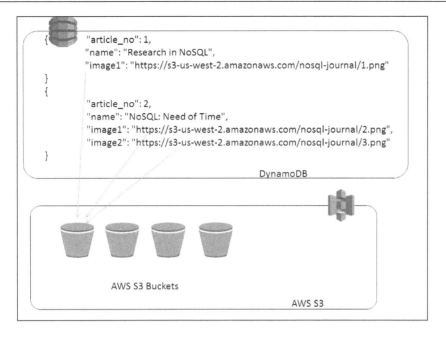

We are going to see more details on AWS S3 integration with DynamoDB in *Chapter 6, Integrating DynamoDB with Other AWS Components*.

Using multiple chunks

There is another good way to store large attribute values—breaking the attribute into multiple chunks and storing them in different DynamoDB tables. You can simply create two tables, one to store the other attribute values and the other to store large attribute values.

An example would be if you want to store blog details in a certain table of DynamoDB, and the blog body might have more data than the maximum allowed size. Then, we create one table called blog to store other blog details and one more table to store blog body.

Blog table

The following is how the blog table would look:

Here blog ID could be the hash key blog ID	Blog name	Number of body chunks
1 '	AWS Best Practices	2
2	DynamoDB Features	2
3	S3 Backup	3

Body chunks table

For the body chunk table, the chunk ID would act as the hash key and could be formed by appending the chunk number to the blog ID.

Chunk ID	Text
1#1	"…AWS Best Practices 1…"
1#2	"…AWS Best Practices 2…"
2#1	"…DynamoDB Features 1…"

Here, we are storing the blog body in multiple chunks. So, when we get a blog item to be stored, we first break the body into multiple chunks and then store the data into respective tables. We can use this batch to get API at the time of retrieval to get the complete body in one go. Here the chunk ID is formed by combining the parent blog ID and the chunk ID.

Please make a note that this technique is feasible only when your attribute value can be broken down into chunks. Also, you might need to spend some time on the data splitting technique, which would also affect the overall time.

Implementing one-to-many relationship

It is recommended to have multiple tables to store items instead of only one. For example, consider the blog table we discussed earlier. There, we might have the comments posted by various readers. We have two choices: first, to store all comments for a related blog in the same table, and second, we can have a separate table with all comments stored for various blogs. Here, if we go with the first option, we might not be able to store all attributes considering the item read and write limitations.

Also, we might not know how many comments we are going to get and what its size would be. So, here it is recommended that we have two separate tables to store the blog and the respective comments on the blogs. Having two tables would also help in isolating faults. Here, if comments tables are throttled, it would not harm the loading of the blog table, hence the recommendation.

There are multiple benefits in having a one-to-many relationship instead of storing everything in one table. The following are some of them:

- Having separate tables for different items helps in maintaining the data as sometimes you might want to retain one but delete the other. In this case, you don't need to delete the complete record; you can simply delete the item you don't wish to see anymore.

- Having multiple tables help us to cater to the size limitation enforced by Amazon. Here, you can have as many comments for a certain blog post, and there would not be any concern about the size limit.

- If we have data stored in separate tables, at the time of querying you can select only the desired data from the desired table instead of fetching all the data for each and every query. This way, you can save money as well as time.

- Also, if we store all comments for a blog post in a single item only, then to retrieve a certain comment you would need to fetch all replies all the time, which is not efficient.

It is also recommended that we have a one-to-many relationship for varied access patterns. This means that if you know that some attributes are required to be fetched more frequently than others, then you should create a table of such items, and you should create another table to store the less-frequently accessed attributes. The reason behind doing this is to fetch data in an efficient manner. This means that if certain attributes are not required most of the time, then if we keep all attributes in one table, we would be unnecessarily fetching them.

Consider an example of the `User` table where we have various attributes, such as first name, last name, e-mail, address, username, password, and so on. We can store all these items together in a table. But we know that username and password are two such important fields that would be used more frequently compared to first name, last name, address, and so on. So, it's efficient to store first name, last name kind of attributes in one table and username and password in another table. So if there are any issues with one of the tables, it would not harm the other table.

Inefficient approach

The following table shows how a user table would look if we keep everything in that table itself.

Table – User

```
{"uid":"111","firstname":"ABC", "lastname":"XYZ",
"address":"St. Paul Street, 11, Oxford", "username":"xyz123",
"password":"xyz@34211", "email":"xyz@pqr.com"}

{"uid":"112", "firstname":"DEF", "lastname":"XYZ",
"address":"St. Paul Street, 12, Oxford", "username":"def123",
"password":def@34211", "email":"def@pqr.com"}
```

Better and efficient approach

As said earlier, if we segregate the credentials from user table, this is how it would look like.

Table – User

```
{"uid":"111", "firstname":"ABC", "lastname":"XYZ",
"address":"St. Paul Street, 11, Oxford", "email":"xyz@pqr.com"}

{"uid":"112", "firstname":"DEF", "lastname":"XYZ",
"address":"St. Paul Street, 12, Oxford", "email":"def@pqr.com"}
```

Table – UserCreds

```
{"uid":"111", "username":"def123", "password":def@34211"}
{"uid":"112", "username":"def123", "password":def@34211"}
```

Query and scan best practices

Query and scan, as we know, are heavy operations and mostly deal with read capacity units provisioned for the particular table. It is very important to take care of even distribution of load considering that the read capacity units get utilized properly. Here are some best practices that you should follow in order to avoid getting exceptions about exceeding provisioned throughput.

Maintaining even read activity

We know that a scan operation fetches 1 MB of data for a single request per page. We also know that an eventually consistent read operation consumes two 4 KB read capacity units per second. This means that a single scan operation costs (1 MB / 4 KB items / two eventually consistent reads) = 128 reads, which would be quite high if you have set your provisioned throughput very low. This sudden burst of data would cause throttling of the provisioned throughput for the given table. Also, meanwhile, if you get a very important request, that request would get throttled after default retries.

Also, it has been observed that scan operations do try to consume capacity units from the same partition that would cause the utilization of all available capacity units for the scan operation only due to which any other request coming to the same partition would not get served. To avoid this, we perform the following operations to maintain the even load distribution for large scan operations.

- We can avoid a sudden burst of large capacity units by reducing the page size. The scan and query operation support the LIMIT attribute, where you can specify the number of items to be retrieved per request. By doing so, there would be some gap between any two page requests, and if there is any other request waiting, then DynamoDB would process that request in between.

- Keeping two tables for the same data is also a good strategy. Here, we can have two tables with the same data, but each one is used for a different purpose. One can be used to dedicatedly do high priority tasks and the other can be used to do queries and scans. So, if by chance, any scan operations get all provisioned throughput, even then you have another table, which would always take care of high-priority or application-critical requests.

But we have to keep in mind that any write operation on a table should also change the values in another table in order to keep in sync.

You should also consider implementing error retries and exponential back-offs so that even if there are more requests coming than the provisioned throughput, all failed requests get retried after an exponential time frame.

Using parallel scans

We have seen in *Chapter 2, Data Models*, about the parallel scan and its advantages. Many times, it is observed that the parallel scan is beneficial as compared with sequential scans. The parallel scan is a good option for all such tables having huge data. We can easily break the data into segments and perform the scan operation. Multiple workers can easily scan the table at low priority, giving way to high priority, thus allowing critical application processes to run smoother.

Even though parallel scans are beneficial, we need to keep in mind that they demand high provisioned throughput. We also need to make sure that worker threads work in such a way that they do not block any other critical processes. In order to help people like us to make decisions about the parallel scan, Amazon has given some directions on when to use parallel scans, which are as follows:

- If the table data size is more than 20 GB
- Table's provisioned throughput capacity is not fully utilized
- Sequential scans are too slow to get the task done

To set a reasonable value to the `TotalSegments` parameter, we need to perform the trial and error method to get the best possible and most efficient way. We can simply start with any number, check the performance, vary the provisioned throughput units, see how they impact the overall performance and cost, and then decide what the perfect number of segments should be.

Local secondary indexes best practices

We have seen what local secondary indexes mean in *Chapter 2, Data Models*. Just to revise, they are secondary indexes that you can define on certain attributes, and which can be used as another range key along with your table hash key. As we have seen, since DynamoDB needs to maintain a complete separate index for these indexes, we have to allocate more resources to it, which makes it a costly affair. So, it is very important to decide on the attribute on which you wish to define the secondary index. It is recommended that the attribute you are not going to query much should not be defined as local secondary index. Indexing should be done for the tables that do not get heavy writes as maintaining those indexes is quite costly.

Indexes should be put on tables that contains sparse data, and which are infrequently updated. It has been observed that the smaller the index, the better the performance. A secondary index consists of an index plus projected attributes. So, it is very important that while creating the index, you should project only required attributes. If a required attribute is not projected in the index, then DynamoDB fetches that attribute from the table, which consumes more read capacity units.

We should also keep a watch every time we update or edit the items in an index. If we don't keep track of the data being written or read, the provisioned throughput capacity would be at risk. We should also keep in mind the maximum item collection (collective size of all items and indexes having same hash key) size limit of 10 GB in the case of local secondary indexes.

Normally, when the item collection size gets exceeded, you get `ItemCollectionSizeLimitExceededException`. The following are some solutions that would help you avoid getting this exception:

- Purging of unnecessary items from the table: This would also delete the respective items from the index as well.

- Updating unnecessary items to remove the projected attributes from the index: This will automatically reduce the size of item collection.

- Backup or moving old data to a new table: It is always a good practice to save historical data in a different table.

Global secondary index best practices

Global secondary indexes allow us to create alternate hash and range keys on non-primary key attributes. Querying is made quite an easy task with secondary indexes. There are various best practices one should follow while using global secondary indexes. We are going to discuss all such best practices in this section.

As we keep saying, it is very important for us to choose the correct hash and range keys attributes, which would be distributing the load evenly across the partitions. We need to choose the attributes having a variety of values as hash and range keys. Consider an example of a student table where we have columns such as roll number, name, grade, and marks. Here, the grade column would have values like A, B, C, and D, while the marks column would have marks obtained by a particular student. Here, we have seen that the grades column has a very limited number of unique values. So, if we create an index on this column, then most of the values would get stored on only a limited number of nodes, which is not a good way to access indexes. Instead, if you put an index on the marks column, the variety of data from that column would help to distribute data evenly across the cluster and hence improve the query performance.

Many people these days use global secondary indexes for quick lookups. Many times, we would have a huge table with large number of attributes attached to each item. Querying such a table is quite an expensive transaction. Also, we might not always need all the attributes given in a certain table. In that case we can create a global secondary index on primary key attributes, adding only required attributes a projected attributes. This technique helps in providing quick lookups with less provisioned throughput, ultimately helping to reduce cost.

We can also create global secondary indexes to store duplicate table data. Here, we can create an index similar to table schema and direct all queries on index instead of table. So, if we are expecting heavy read/write operations on the table, then regular queries can be directed to indexes. This would allow us to keep the provisioned throughput constant for the table and also avoid a sudden burst, keeping all table transactions intact.

We should make a note that **Global Secondary Indexes** (**GSI**) are eventually consistent, which means an under-provisioned GSI can have a huge impact on table write throughput, and it may also lead us to exceed the provisioned throughput. To know more about this, you can go through the `https://forums.aws.amazon.com/thread.jspa?threadID=143009` thread.

Summary

In this chapter, we have gone through some best practices that one should follow in order to get the maximum out of DynamoDB. We started with table best practices where we talked about how to choose correct primary keys, how to create table schemas, how to manage the time series data, and so on. In item best practices, we talked about caching, storing large attributes, one-to- many data modeling, and so on. In query and scan best practices, we saw how to maintain even data load to improve query performance. We also discussed the use of parallel scans and its benefits.

In the last section, we talked about local and global secondary best practices. A good understanding of DynamoDB architecture would help you to find more such best practices, which in turn would help you reduce cost and improve performance. So keep learning and keep exploring.

In the next chapter, we will cover some advanced topics, such as DynamoDB monitoring, common useful tools, libraries, AWS authentication service, and error handling.

5
Advanced Topics

In the previous chapter, we talked about the best practices one should follow in order to get the most out of DynamoDB. In this chapter, we are going to talk about some advanced topics:

- Monitoring DynamoDB tables
- AWS authentication service
- AWS IAM integration with DynamoDB
- Security token service
- Error handling in DynamoDB

We will also talk about limitations of DynamoDB that every developer needs to consider while designing the schema and doing the implementation.

Monitoring DynamoDB tables

To start with, let's get familiar with AWS CloudWatch, which is a network-monitoring service offered by Amazon Web Service. While creating a table, you can set alarms for various events such as provisioning a throughput with exceeded exceptions, maintaining certain threshold, and so on. A table's size in terms of bytes or number of items is not available as a CloudWatch metric by default; however, this can be set up using the `DescribeTable` operation, and it is a good practice to keep watch on this metric. These metrics are very important from the database admin's point of view, but as we are using a hosted service here, we need not hire a DBA specialist. These metrics would help us keep track of whether there is any sudden demand of resources happening or not, and if the peak and slow time frames can be drawn for our application so that we can keep more read and write throughput for peak time frames and lesser throughput for slow time frames. CloudWatch gives us a detailed report of the metrics we want to monitor.

There are various ways of monitoring DynamoDB tables using CloudWatch as follows:

- AWS Management Console
- API
- Command-line interface

AWS Management Console

This is the easiest and simplest way of monitoring DynamoDB tables. By default, you can see table-related metrics once you select the table in question in AWS Management Console. To get table-related metrics, you can go to the AWS CloudWatch management console URL at `https://console.aws.amazon.com/ cloudwatch/`.

There, on the left-hand side, you need to click on the **Metrics** pane to view the list of available metrics. Once you're there, you can simply select DynamoDB metrics, as shown in the following screenshot:

When you click on it, you will get a list of metrics for your tables and secondary indexes, if any, as shown in the following screenshot:

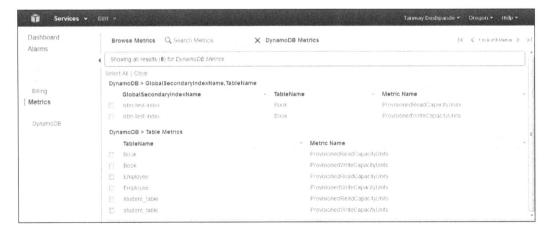

Now if you click on any metrics, you will be able to see their graphs, as shown in the following screenshot. You can also view historic data to understand the usage pattern of the application and then decide on tuning the read and write capacity units for that particular table.

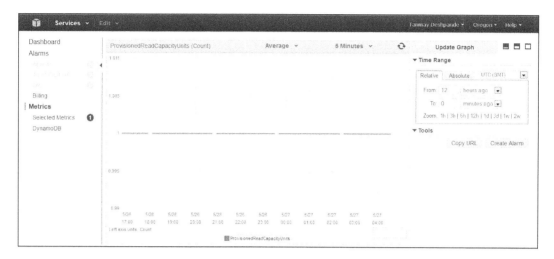

Here, I have selected metrics for the table Book to understand the read capacity unit usage.

CloudWatch API

CloudWatch provides us with a query API in order to get DynamoDB metrics programmatically. For this, you need to provide valid data in a query format and simply hit the request with proper credentials. A simple query normally looks for information such as the table name, operation (`getItem`, `putItem`, and so on), time frame (start time and end time), and so on. A typical query request will look as follows:

```
http://monitoring.amazonaws.com/
    ?SignatureVersion=2
    &Action=ReturnedItemCount
    &Version=2010-08-01
    &StartTime=2014-04-14T00:00:00
    &EndTime=2014-05-16T00:00:00
    &Period=500
    &Statistics.member.1=Sum
    &Dimensions.member.1=Operation=Scan,TableName=Book
    &Namespace=AWS/DynamoDB
    &MetricName=ReturnedItemCount
    &Timestamp=2014-04-28T14%3A48%3A11.876Z
    &AWSAccessKeyId=<Access Key>
    &Signature=<Signature>
```

Depending on the need, you can select the required metrics and appropriate operations. There is a list of DynamoDB metrics and dimensions for those metrics; go through `http://docs.aws.amazon.com/AmazonCloudWatch/latest/DeveloperGuide/dynamo-metricscollected.html` to get more details on this.

A command-line interface

CloudWatch also provides a command-line interface to retrieve metrics about DynamoDB tables and its operations. To use it, you need to first install the command-line tool on your machine, as described in the CloudWatch developer guide at `http://docs.aws.amazon.com/AmazonCloudWatch/latest/cli/SetupCLI.html`.

Like the CloudWatch API, we need to provide correct information to the command-line tool to get more information. We need to provide the metrics name and the dimension associated with it, as shown in the following command:

```
cmd>mon-get-stats ThrottledRequests --aws-credential-file ./<AWS_CREDS_
FILE_PATH>.template --namespace "AWS/DynamoDB"

--statistics "Sum" --start-time 2014-04-14T00:00:00Z --end-time
2014-05-16T00:00:00Z --period 500 --dimensions "Operation=Scan"
```

Many times it happens that the senior management of your organization wants to have a look at the application's performance. So, the only way to show them the reports is to give them access to the AWS management console, which is a quite a risky thing to do, considering their non-technical background. Therefore, in order to solve this problem, you can create your own monitoring portal where you can use CloudWatch APIs or CI to get the data on the fly without sharing AWS credentials with any non-technical person and still display the results.

Using IAM to provide access control to DynamoDB

Some of you might be aware of the concept called access control on resources. This is a very familiar concept in relational databases where we can have multiple users accessing the same database but different roles. This is very crucial from the application's security point of view. A user should have privileges and access to only the required resources in order to avoid misuse. In order to implement the concept on Cloud, AWS supports **Identity and Access Management (IAM)** as a service. This service allows us to perform the following:

- Create multiple AWS accounts that access the same resources with different privileges
- Create group users with similar privileges for the same level of accesses
- Create separate user credentials for each user and maintain privacy
- Provide fine-grained control on shared resources
- Get a collective bill for all the users under one account

We can use IAM to control DynamoDB resources and API accesses to users. To do so, you need to create an IAM policy that would list down details about the policy, such as what permission does this user have on a certain table, whether a particular group can edit/delete a record from a table, and so on. For example, you can create a table, say Author, in your account and then create a policy document describing its access definitions. Once done, you can apply that policy on certain IAM users that would restrict them to their defined roles. Suppose you have provided read-only access to the user Jack, then he would only be able to read the Author table and would not be able to edit/delete anything from it.

How to use IAM for DynamoDB

Now let's try to understand the creation of access control in a stepwise manner. To begin, you need to go to the IAM console page first at `https://console.aws.amazon.com/iam/`.

You will see a console and a button **Create New Group of Users**, as shown in the following screenshot:

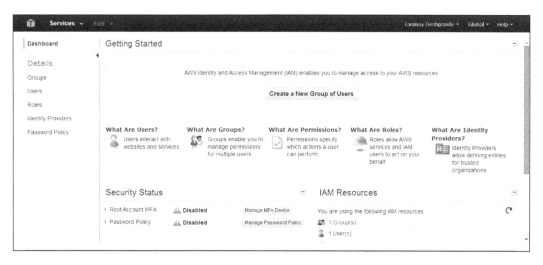

If you press this button, you will get a pop-up asking you to name the new group, as shown in the following screenshot. Here, I am naming the group `read-only-group`.

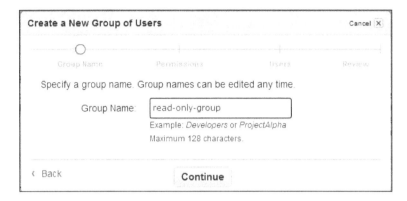

Once you click on **Continue**, you will see a policy selection window where you can simply select preconfigured templates or create custom policies. Here, I am selecting the **Policy Generator** option, as shown in the following screenshot:

In the policy generator, I am asking AWS to provide all of the read rights to this group, as shown in the following screenshot. Here, you also need to specify the ARN of the resource where you need to apply these policies. Let's apply these policies to the Employee table that we created earlier.

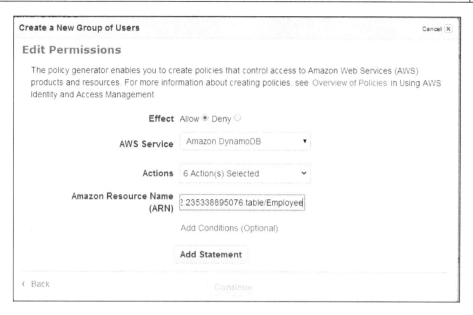

Once you click on **Add Statement**, the **Continue** button will be enabled. When you click on it, you will be able to see the policy document. You can also edit the policy name, as shown in the following screenshot:

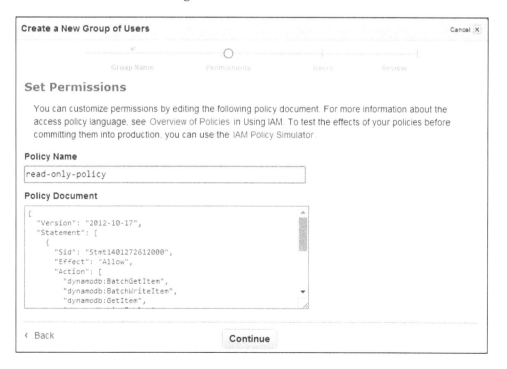

The next thing we need to do is add users to the read-only group. You can add new or existing users. Here, I am adding an existing user:

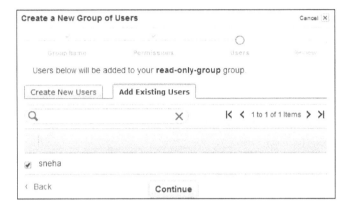

Once done, you can review and submit the group created. Now that we have given read-only rights to this group, you can verify the same by logging in as the new user:

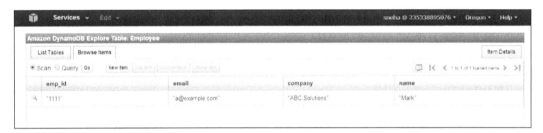

In the previous screenshot, you can see that I have logged in as a newly created user, and I am able to read the Employee table. Now if I try to add a new item by performing a `PutItem` request, I would not be able to do so as it is unauthorized:

Note that before we apply this policy, you should add one more policy that will allow new users to access the DynamoDB console using the following policy document so that you won't be surprised to see a **Not Authorized** message on the DynamoDB console.

```
{
    "Version": "2012-10-17",
    "Statement": [
        {
            "Action": [
                "cloudwatch:DescribeAlarms",
                "cloudwatch:ListMetrics",
"dynamodb:DescribeTable",
                "dynamodb:ListTables"
            ],
            "Effect": "Allow",
            "Resource": "*"
        }
    ]
}
```

Also, don't forget to add the given user to the newly created group.

Sample IAM policies

In this section, we will try to list some sample IAM policies that would be helpful to you. We have already one example policy document that enables users to view the AWS DynamoDB console. Now let's try to explore more of these policy documents.

Providing read-only access to items from all DynamoDB tables

To read items, there are only two APIs called `GetItem` and `BatchGetItem`. So in this document, we are allowing only those actions for all the tables, as shown in the following code:

```
{
    "Version": "2012-10-17",       # Version of AWS API
    "Statement": [
        {
            "Effect": "Allow",     # Allow means enable the below given
operations
```

```
          "Action": [
              "dynamodb:GetItem",      # DynamoDB operations to be
    considered
              "dynamodb:BatchGetItem"
          ],
          "Resource": "*"      # Any AWS resource, here it means all
    DynamoDB tables
        }
    ]
}
```

Restrict users from deleting all the tables and items from a table

In this policy, we are restricting any delete action that comes to DynamoDB from any user. The statement for the same would look as the following code:

```
{
  "Version": "2012-10-17",
  "Statement": [{
    "Effect": "Deny",
    "Action": ["dynamodb:DeleteItem",
    "dynamodb:DeleteTable"],
    "Resource": ["*"]
  }]
}
```

Allowing you to place and update an item on a single table

In the following code, we are creating a statement that will allow all the users under this group to add a new item to the table Employee and update any existing items in the same table:

```
{
  "Version": "2012-10-17",
  "Statement": [{
    "Effect": "Allow",
    "Action": ["dynamodb:PutItem",
    "dynamodb:UpdateItem"],
    "Resource": ["arn:aws:dynamodb:us-west-2:235338895076:table/
Employee"]
  }]
}
```

Please make sure that you change the resource ARN as per your table details.

Allowing access to all indexes of a particular table

Here, we will need to provide all the permissions to the `Employee` table's indexes. To access the indexes of a table, we just need to add `/index/*` after the table ARN. In order to access a specific index, you can mention the index name such as `/index/<index-name>`. The following is a statement that provides all the permissions to every index of the `Employee` table:

```
{
  "Version": "2012-10-17",
  "Statement": [{
    "Effect": "Allow",
    "Action": ["dynamodb:*"],
    "Resource": ["arn:aws:dynamodb:us-west-2:235338895076:table/
Employee/index/*"]
  }]
}
```

Allowing all DynamoDB actions to all the tables

If you want to provide all of the accesses to the users of all the tables, then you need to create a policy document, as shown in the following code:

```
{
  "Version": "2012-10-17",
  "Statement": [
    {

    "Effect": "Allow",
      "Action": [
        "dynamodb:*"
      ],
      "Resource": [
        "*"
      ]
    }
  ]
}
```

By this time, you will have figured out how easy it is to create policy documents and apply the same on required groups. As shown earlier, you can simply use a policy generator provided by AWS to play around with different policies.

Fine-grained access control

In the earlier section, we saw how to restrict users from using a certain API or not allowing some other API. However, there might be some use cases where you need to restrict certain users from having access to item-level data. For all such cases, DynamoDB has provided fine-grained access control on each and every item of DynamoDB tables. There could be lots of places in your application where you would like to restrict users from accessing the information as follows:

- In the `Employee` table, the employee name, address, and telephone number should be visible to all the users, but the salary of an employee should be visible to only the concerned users. This is a good example of vertical access control where each row represents a separate user.

- Also if x number of employees report to manager A and y number of employees report to manager B, then both manager A and B should be able to view details about their direct reports. Here again, we assume that each row in a DynamoDB table represents a single employee. We can control or restrict the access of managers to only their direct reports.

To do such things, we can use the same policy documents, adding appropriate control statements. You can add horizontal and vertical access controls to those statements and verify the same using examples.

To understand horizontal and vertical access controls, let's continue with our `Employee` table example where we have an `Employee` table that has stored information of all the employees. Now we will be creating a policy document that will let employees access only their personal information and also restrict them from accessing sensitive information such as performance rating, but allowing rest all attributes to be accessed. The following is a policy document for the same:

```
{
    "Version": "2012-10-17",
    "Statement": [
        {
            "Effect": "Allow",
            "Action": [
                "dynamodb:GetItem",
                "dynamodb:BatchGetItem",
                "dynamodb:Query",
                "dynamodb:PutItem",
                "dynamodb:UpdateItem",
                "dynamodb:DeleteItem",
                "dynamodb:BatchWriteItem"
            ],
```

```
        "Resource": [
            "arn:aws:dynamodb:us-west-2:235338895076:table/
Employee"
        ],
        "Condition": {
            "ForAllValues:StringEquals": {
                "dynamodb:LeadingKeys":  ["${www.amazon.com:user_
id}"],
                "dynamodb:Attributes": [
                    "user_id", "emp_id", "email", "company" ,
"salary" , "name"
                ]
            },
            "StringEqualsIfExists": {"dynamodb:Select": "SPECIFIC_
ATTRIBUTES"}
        }
    }
  ]
}
```

We have put in the following two conditions:

- To restrict users to access only their information, we have added a condition to show the row information of the matching user_id only. Here, user_id is fetched from the variable www.amazon.com:user_id that checks with web identity federation user ID, that is, Amazon, Google, or Facebook's user ID. If it matches, only then the matching row information will be displayed.

- To restrict users from accessing sensitive information such as performance rating, we have added another condition to show only the given list of attributes to be shown at any get call.

Here, the first condition allows us to implement horizontal restrictions, while the second condition allows us to implement vertical access control. Again, to build the policy document, you can use a policy generator UI provided by AWS.

 Whenever you use dynamodb:attributes or not, you must specify all the primary key and index key attributes in the list. If you don't provide this information, DynamoDB will not be able use those hash and range indexes to get the expected response.

Sample fine-grained access control policies

Now let's try to list down the commonly used fine-grained access control policies that can be used as a reference by you.

Restricting access to only specific hash value

This is a very popular use case where you want the user data in your table to be accessed by only the respected users. The following is the policy statement for the same:

```
{
    "Version": "2012-10-17",
    "Statement": [
        {
            "Effect": "Allow",
            "Action": [
                "dynamodb:GetItem",
                "dynamodb:BatchGetItem",
                "dynamodb:Query",
                "dynamodb:PutItem",
                "dynamodb:UpdateItem",
                "dynamodb:DeleteItem",
                "dynamodb:BatchWriteItem"
            ],
            "Resource": ["arn:aws:dynamodb:us-west-
2:235338895076:table/Employee"],
            "Condition": {
                "ForAllValues:StringEquals": {"dynamodb:LeadingKeys":
["${www.amazon.com:user_id}"]}
            }
        }
    ]
}
```

Restricting access to only specific attributes of a table

This is a vertical access control policy that limits users from accessing certain attributes of a table. For example, in the case of the `Employee` table, we would be restricting users from accessing information such as performance rating and so on, using the following code:

```
{
    "Version": "2012-10-17",
    "Statement": [
        {
            "Effect": "Allow",
            "Action": [
                "dynamodb:GetItem",
                "dynamodb:Query",
                "dynamodb:BatchGetItem",
                "dynamodb:Scan",
        "dynamodb:UpdateItem"
            ],
            "Resource": ["arn:aws:dynamodb:us-west-
2:235338895076:table/Employee"],
            "Condition": {
                "ForAllValues:StringEquals": {
                    "dynamodb:Attributes": ["user_id","name","email",
"address"]]
                },
                "StringEqualsIfExists": {
                    "dynamodb:Select": "SPECIFIC_ATTRIBUTES",
                    "dynamodb:ReturnValues": [
                        "NONE",
                        "UPDATED_OLD",
                        "UPDATED_NEW"
                    ]
                }
            }
        }
    ]
}
```

This policy restricts users from accessing information only associated with their user ID. Also, it allows users to access only the user_id, name, email and address attributes to be retrieved and updated. It does not allow them to add a new item or delete an existing one.

The second condition allows users to return only specific attributes if he or she uses the Select statement. It also provides information on what needs to return in the case of an Update statement.

Allowing a query on only specific projected attributes in index

In this document, we will try to create a policy statement that would allow users to see only specific attributes projected in a secondary index. Here, we would use a secondary index called `PayScaleIndex` for our purpose, which is part of the `Employee` table:

```
{
    "Version": "2012-10-17",
    "Statement": [
        {
            "Effect": "Allow",
            "Action": ["dynamodb:Query"],
            "Resource": ["arn:aws:dynamodb:us-west-
2:235338895076:table/Employee/index/PayScaleIndex"],
            "Condition": {
                "ForAllValues:StringEquals": {
                    "dynamodb:Attributes": [
                        "salary" , "grade", "bonus"
                    ]
                },
                "StringEquals": {"dynamodb:Select": "SPECIFIC_
ATTRIBUTES"}
            }
        }
    ]
}
```

Similarly, you can create your own policy documents to fit your needs and apply the same on users.

Web identity federation

By now, you would have started thinking of how to apply access controls on application that have a huge number of users. There, it is not possible to create policies for individual users as and when they are getting created. To solve this issue, AWS offers one unique way that would allow you to let users use their social media credentials, for example, the ones used for Facebook, Google, or Amazon to use the application. Here, the identity of the users would be provided by identity providers such as Google, Facebook, or Amazon, and authentication and authorization is performed by providing these users with a simple secure token. AWS supports the growing number of identity providers such as the following:

- Google
- Facebook
- Amazon

Web identity federation is very helpful for an application where the number of users are expected to be more. A good example would be an online dating or gaming site.

The web identity federation is shown in the following diagram:

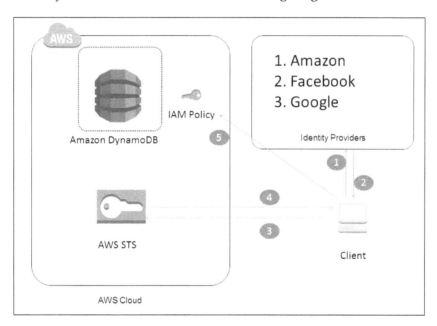

The web identity federation involves the following things:

1. The client application asks the user to log in with any of the identity providers and then sends the information to the identity provider for verification.
2. In response, the identity provider sends a web identity token to the client.
3. The app then calls the AWS STS service, sending the web identity as the input.
4. AWS STS generates a temporary AWS credential token for the client and sends it back to it with some role attached to the token/user.
5. The app then calls DynamoDB to access the desired table. Depending on the policy details, IAM decides whether the access is granted or not. The policy statement is the same as the one we have seen in last couple of sections.

This way, using web identity federation, you can handle authorization and authentication of users for applications with a large number of user base.

Limitations in DynamoDB

In this section, we will try to list the limitations put by AWS on DynamoDB operations. These limits need to be considered while using DynamoDB in order to keep your application 100 percent available without any hiccups.

Attribute	Limitation Details
Table name/index name	Table/index name can contain A-Z, a-z, 0-9, underscore (_), dash (-) and dot (.). The table name should be a minimum of 3 and maximum of 255 characters. There is no limit on the table name that starts with the previously mentioned special characters.
Tables per account	You can create a maximum of 256 tables per region through one account.
Table size	There is no limit on the number of items or size of the table in terms of bytes.
Hash key	There is no limit on the number of hash keys in a table.
Range key	There is no limit on the number of range keys per unique hash key for tables without a local secondary index. For a table with a local secondary index, the total size of the table, including the indexes, should not exceed 10 GB.
Number of secondary indexes per table	There is a limit of five local and five global secondary indexes per table.
Number of projected attributes	There is a maximum limit of 20 attributes on a local secondary index that is created by the user.
Primary key attribute name	The name should be of 1 to 255 characters in length. It should only use the character that can be encoded by UTF-8 encoders.
Item size	The item's size should be less than or equal to 64 KB. The item's size is calculated considering both the attribute name and its value in the case of each attribute.
Attribute values	Attribute values cannot be null or empty.
Primary key attribute value—Hash key	The maximum allowed size is 2048 bytes.

Attribute	Limitation Details
Primary key attribute value — Range key	The maximum allowed size is 1024 bytes.
Query	The query result set should not be of more than 1 MB.
Scan	The scan data result set should not exceed size restrictions of 1 MB.
BatchGetItem	`BatchGetItem` can fetch 100 items at a time, provided the total item size does not exceed 1 MB.
BatchWriteItem	Up to 25 `PutItem` or `DeleteItem` requests can be fired without exceeding the data size limit of 1 MB.
Data type — String	All the strings should be according to UTF-8 encoding.
Data type — Number	A number can have up to 38 digit precision.
Provisioned throughput limit	For US East Region, a table can scale up to 40,000 read or write capacity units, and for the rest of regions, DynamoDB tables can scale up to 10000 read/write capacity units per table.

These limits do not mean that DynamoDB has technical limitations in it. However, these limits are put in order to maintain the multi-tenant infrastructure and to avoid any misuse of the complete infrastructure by a single user or group of users.

Error handling

In this section, we are going to talk about how to handle errors in DynamoDB. We have seen how to make client requests in earlier chapters of this book. There, we had not put the error-handling mechanism, which we would be doing now.

Type of errors

There are two types of errors in AWS:

- Client errors: These normally come when the request we are submitting is incorrect. The client errors are normally shown with the status code starting with 4XX. These errors normally arrive when there is an authentication failure, bad requests, missing required attributes, or for exceeding the provisioned throughput. The errors normally come when users provide invalid inputs.

- Server errors: These arrive when there is something wrong from Amazon's side, and they appear at runtime. The only way to handle such errors is to try again, and even then if it does not succeed, then you should log the request ID and reach Amazon support with that ID to know more about the details.

You can get the full list of AWS DynamoDB error code and the description at `http://docs.aws.amazon.com/amazondynamodb/latest/developerguide/ErrorHandling.html#APIError`.

Catching error information

This is as important as handling the error. When it comes to Java, you should always write the request in `try` or `catch` blocks. In a `try` block, you can invoke the request, and in a `catch` block, you can catch `AmazonServiceException` first and then `AmazonClientException`. You can perform the process of catching an error using the following code:

```
        try{
        // Scan items for all values
        ScanRequest scanRequest = new ScanRequest("Employee");
        ScanResult scanResult = dynamoDBClient.scan(scanRequest);

    }
catch(AmazonServiceException ase){
        System.err.println("Failed scan table: " + "Employee");
            // Get detail error information
            System.out.println("Error Message:    " + ase.getMessage());
            System.out.println("HTTP Status Code: " + ase.
getStatusCode());
            System.out.println("AWS Error Code:   " + ase.
getErrorCode());
            System.out.println("Error Type:       " + ase.
getErrorType());
            System.out.println("Request ID:       " + ase.
getRequestId());
    }

catch (AmazonClientException e) {
    System.out.println("Amazon Client Exception :"+e.getMessage());

}
```

As I said earlier, it is very important to make a note of the request ID if you need to go back to Amazon support to perform more digging into the error.

Auto retries and exponential back-offs

In the case of client errors, we can put some code around autoerror retries. Sometimes, it's possible that your provisioned throughput is utilized to the maximum; in this case, it's good to perform autoerror retries. The simplest way of performing this is using the client configuration provided by Amazon, as shown in the following code:

```
ClientConfiguration configuration = new ClientConfiguration();
configuration.setMaxErrorRetry(3);
// Instantiate AWS Client with proper credentials and client
configuration
dynamoDBClient = new AmazonDynamoDBClient(
new ClasspathPropertiesFileCredentialsProvider(), configuration);
```

Here, you can set the number as per your need. By default, Amazon has put some autoerror retries policies that you can see from the Amazon SDK code, which is of 20,000 milliseconds, and the maximum error retries is three.

The Amazon SDK also allows you to create your own back-off policy, as shown in the following code:

```
ClientConfiguration configuration = new ClientConfiguration();

RetryPolicy policy = new RetryPolicy(retryCondition, backoffStrategy,
maxErrorRetry, honorMaxErrorRetryInClientConfig);

configuration.setRetryPolicy(retryPolicy);

// Instantiate AWS Client with proper credentials and client
configuration
dynamoDBClient = new AmazonDynamoDBClient(
new ClasspathPropertiesFileCredentialsProvider(), configuration);
```

Some terms in the previous code are explained as follows:

- `RetryCondition`: Here, you need to specify whether on a specific request or condition, if you need to retry. If null is specified, then SDK takes the default condition.

- `BackoffStrategy`: Here, you need to specify after how long the next retry should be done. If null is specified, then SDK takes the default strategy.

- `MaxErrorRetry`: Here, you need to specify the maximum number of retries on the error.

- `HonorMaxErrorRetryInClientConfig`: Here, you need to specify whether this retry policy should honor the max error retry set by `ClientConfiguration.setMaxErrorRetry(int)`.

If required, you can also use a custom retry strategy, or you can also use AWS SQS to throttle the DynamoDB throughput. Use the `http://tech.shazam.com/server/using-sqs-to-throttle-dynamodb-throughput/` blog link that explains the detailed implementation for the same.

Summary

In this chapter, we started with understanding how to monitor DynamoDB tables; we saw various ways of the DynamoDB status and how to use it to get correct information about DynamoDB all the time. Then, we started with the AWS security model for DynamoDB. There, we talked about implementing security policies based on user roles and applying the same to the application. We went through a stepwise tutorial to create security groups, policies, and applying them on sample DynamoDB tables.

We also went through multiple example security policies, which would help to build a secure app in the near future. We also understood how to create fine-grained access control in real-time applications to maintain the integrity of the system. We also learned about one very interesting topic called web identity federation where we can use third-party websites to use the user identity and allow them to connect to DynamoDB after a successful token verification.

Finally, we listed down the best practices of limitations and error handling in DynamoDB, which one should keep handy in order to design a hiccup-free system.

In the next chapter, we will talk about how to integrate DynamoDB with other AWS components in order to build the complete application ecosystem within cloud.

6
Integrating DynamoDB with Other AWS Components

This is an era of ecosystems. Everyone wants all their things to be at one place, and there is absolutely nothing wrong with it as, if we get all that we need at one place, it becomes quite easy to manage our stuff. Consider an example of the supermarket; we like to go to the supermarket instead of individual store keepers as we get all that we need at one place. The same is the case with technology, we normally prefer to use libraries from some particular companies only, because it provides great compatibility, ease of integration, and ease of moving from one component to another as the same conventions and styles would be used to develop it.

When Amazon understood this need, they started offering a variety of technologies as a service on cloud. For example, they started with S3; then, they realized offering EC2 instances would also be a good idea and since then their offering stack is evolving every day. Right from the **relational database (RDS)** to the NoSQL database (DynamoDB), from workflow (SWF) to a search engine (CloudSearch), and from Hadoop (EMR) to **Identity and Access Management (IAM)**, you name it and Amazon has already provided all it takes to build the end-to-end application system. In this chapter, we will see how to integrate DynamoDB with other AWS offerings so that you are able to develop a complete application on AWS Cloud itself. We will cover the integration of DynamoDB with the following tools:

- **Elastic MapReduce (EMR)**
- **Simple Storage Service (S3)**
- RedShift
- CloudSearch

Integrating with AWS EMR

Hadoop and Big Data is one of the most used extract, transform, and load (ETL) tools these days. Most of the companies are using it to fetch more and more information from the data available with them. But sometimes it is found that creating and maintaining the Hadoop cluster is quite a time-consuming job, especially when you don't have much exposure to the Linux/Unix environment. Also, if you need to use Hadoop in production, you would need to hire a specialist Hadoop admin, which is an overhead in terms of cost. To solve this, AWS has introduced a hosted Hadoop as a service where you just need to provide your requirement in terms of cluster configuration (number of data nodes and the size of instances based on the size of data you want to process), additional services such as Hive, Pig, and so on, if required, and once done, on a single click of the button, you have your Hadoop cluster ready.

You can find more details about how to launch Elastic MapReduce EMR cluster and how to play with it at `http://docs.aws.amazon.com/ElasticMapReduce/latest/DeveloperGuide/emr-what-is-emr.html`.

In this section, we will cover the following topics:

- Exporting data from DynamoDB
- Querying and joining tables in DynamoDB using AWS EMR
- Importing data to DynamoDB

Exporting data from DynamoDB

There might be many places where your application data that is stored in DynamoDB needs to be exported to flat files. This exercise could be a part of data archiving, data purging, or some data movement. Even when you need to perform data analytics on DynamoDB data using EMR you can either first export it to S3 or to **Hadoop Distributed File System (HDFS)**. Now let's learn how to export data to S3/HDFS in a stepwise manner.

The pre-requisites to perform this exercise are as follows:

- An EMR Hadoop cluster with Hive installed
- A simple AWS S3 bucket
- A DynamoDB table with some data to be exported
- Knowledge of HiveQL/Hadoop

Export data to AWS S3

AWS S3 is a cheaper way to store or dump your data. Amazon allows us to export data from DynamoDB quite easily. We can export data to S3 in various forms, such as simple data (as it is), formatted data, or compressed data. We can perform them by using simple data export.

Consider that you have a table called Employee that contains data about employee details. A schema for the table would be something like this: Employee (empId:String, yoj:String, dept:String, salary:Number, manager:String).

Suppose we decide to export the data from this table to a bucket called packt-pub-employee in the folder /employee_data, then, you can write a Hive query to first create a hive table as shown by the following commands:

```
CREATE EXTERNAL TABLE packtPubEmployee (empid String, yoj String,
department String, salary bigint, ,manager String)
STORED BY 'org.apache.hadoop.hive.dynamodb.DynamoDBStorageHandler'
TBLPROPERTIES ("dynamodb.table.name" = "Employee",
"dynamodb.column.mapping" = "empid:empId,yoj:yoj,department:dept,salary:s
alary,manager:manager");
```

Here, we are creating an external Hive table called packtPubEmployee with the same schema as the DynamoDB table. By providing TBLPROPERTIES for this table, we are indicating which table from DynamoDB is to be mapped to this table in Hive and what columns are to be mapped from DynamoDB table to hive table.

Once you run this on Hive by connecting to the EMR cluster, the table definition would get created; the actual data exporting would happen once you run the following HiveQL statement, which will run the insert data statement:

```
INSERT OVERWRITE DIRECTORY 's3://packt-pub-employee/employee/' SELECT *
FROM packtPubEmployee;
```

Here, you can replace your own bucket path instead of mine, and the same is the case with the DynamoDB table name. Once you run this statement, EMR will launch a MapReduce job, which would take its own time depending upon the data it needs to process. Once done, you can check the S3 bucket, and you would be able to see the data from DynamoDB stored in flat files.

Formatted data export

If you want to export specific columns from the table, then you can simply mention them in the SELECT statement. For example, if you want to export only employee ID and salary, then you can rewrite the insert statement as follows:

```
INSERT OVERWRITE DIRECTORY 's3://packt-pub-employee/employee/' SELECT
empid, salary

FROM packtPubEmployee;
```

But make sure you make corresponding changes in the Hive table as well. You can also export data specifying some formatting in between the columns. Formatting generally helps when you need to export a table with some delimiters. The following is an example where we are exporting the same Employee table with tab-delimited columns:

```
CREATE EXTERNAL TABLE packtPubEmployee (empid String, yoj String,
department String, salary bigint, ,manager String)

STORED BY 'org.apache.hadoop.hive.dynamodb.DynamoDBStorageHandler'

TBLPROPERTIES ("dynamodb.table.name" = "Employee",

"dynamodb.column.mapping" =
"empid:empId,yoj:yoj,department:dept,salary:salary,manager:manager");


CREATE EXTERNAL TABLE packtPubEmployee_tab_formatted(a_col string, b_col
bigint, c_col array<string>)

ROW FORMAT DELIMITED FIELDS TERMINATED BY '\t'

LOCATION 's3://packt-pub-employee/employee/';


INSERT OVERWRITE TABLE packtPubEmployee_tab_formatted SELECT *

FROM packtPubEmployee;
```

Here, the only change we need to make is create one staging table with the row format delimiter specified.

Compressed data export

Most of the time, we do data export to archive old data on S3. This kind of data is not frequently used but needs to be kept somewhere so that in case it is needed, it can be taken out. Hadoop/Hive supports various data compression algorithms. So, you can decide which algorithm to use to store data in compressed manner. The following example demonstrates how to export DynamoDB data to AWS S3 in compressed flat files.

To do so, you just need to set certain property values in the Hive console before you run the export job. Here is a sample Hive script that exports data from the DynamoDB table called `Employee` to S3 bucket in compressed files:

```
SET hive.exec.compress.output=true; # Sets the compression mode ON.

SET io.seqfile.compression.type=BLOCK; # Sets the type of compression

SET mapred.output.compression.codec = org.apache.hadoop.io.compress.
GzipCodec;

# Sets the algorithm to be used for compression.


CREATE EXTERNAL TABLE packtPubEmployee (empid String, yoj String,
department String, salary bigint, ,manager String)

STORED BY 'org.apache.hadoop.hive.dynamodb.DynamoDBStorageHandler'

TBLPROPERTIES ("dynamodb.table.name" = "Employee",

"dynamodb.column.mapping" =
"empid:empId,yoj:yoj,department:dept,salary:salary,manager:manager");


CREATE EXTERNAL TABLE packtPubEmployee_tab_formatted(a_col string, b_col
bigint, c_col array<string>)

ROW FORMAT DELIMITED FIELDS TERMINATED BY '\t'

LOCATION 's3://packt-pub-employee/employee/';


INSERT OVERWRITE TABLE packtPubEmployee_tab_formatted SELECT *

FROM packtPubEmployee;
```

Here we are using gzip codec from Hadoop to compress the files. The other available codecs are as follows:

- `org.apache.hadoop.io.compress.DefaultCodec`
- `com.hadoop.compression.lzo.LzoCodec`
- `org.apache.hadoop.io.compress.BZip2Codec`
- `org.apache.hadoop.io.compress.SnappyCodec`

Export data to EMR – HDFS

We can also export the DynamoDB table data to certain folder on **Hadoop Distributed File System** (**HDFS**). There might be a use case where you would need to process data on Hadoop using a MapReduce job instead of directly running a Hive query. In this case, we would first need to get the data in some HDFS folder and then run the MapReduce job on it. The following code script represents the importing data from DynamoDB table to HDFS:

```
CREATE EXTERNAL TABLE packtPubEmployee (empid String, yoj String,
department String, salary bigint, ,manager String)

STORED BY 'org.apache.hadoop.hive.dynamodb.DynamoDBStorageHandler'

TBLPROPERTIES ("dynamodb.table.name" = "Employee",

"dynamodb.column.mapping" =
"empid:empId,yoj:yoj,department:dept,salary:salary,manager:manager");


SET dynamodb.throughput.read.percent=1.0;


INSERT OVERWRITE DIRECTORY 'hdfs:///data/employee/' SELECT * FROM
packtPubEmployee;
```

Here, by setting the `dynamodb.throughput.read.percent` variable, we are controlling the read request rate from DynamoDB; you can play around with this variable value and tune it to make it suitable for your performance expectations. In the insert query, you need to specify the directory on HDFS where you wish to export the data. This would also allow us to export data from production DynamoDB table without risking a performance degrade.

Querying DynamoDB data

Querying data using SQL in DynamoDB is one the main reasons why we integrate DynamoDB with EMR. To perform the same, we just need to map DynamoDB table attributes with a hive table, and once done, you can simply write your own queries in Hive in order to get the desired output. The following are some sample examples that would help you to form your own queries.

Getting the total count of employees in Employee table

To get the count of employees from DynamoDB table `Employee`, we first need to create a table with mappings in Hive. Once the table is created, you can simply run the `count(*)` query to get the exact count of employees.

```
CREATE EXTERNAL TABLE packtPubEmployee (empid String, yoj String,
department String, salary bigint, manager String)

STORED BY 'org.apache.hadoop.hive.dynamodb.DynamoDBStorageHandler'

TBLPROPERTIES ("dynamodb.table.name" = "Employee",

"dynamodb.column.mapping" =
"empid:empId,yoj:yoj,department:dept,salary:salary,manager:manager");


SELECT COUNT(*) FROM packtPubEmployee;
```

Getting the total count of employees department wise

Here, we would need to GROUP BY employees according to their department. The steps are simple: create a table with attribute mappings and then fire a SELECT query to GROUP BY employees to get their count. Have a look at the following commands:

```
CREATE EXTERNAL TABLE packtPubEmployee (empid String, yoj String,
department String, salary bigint, ,manager String)

STORED BY 'org.apache.hadoop.hive.dynamodb.DynamoDBStorageHandler'

TBLPROPERTIES ("dynamodb.table.name" = "Employee",

"dynamodb.column.mapping" =
"empid:empId,yoj:yoj,department:dept,salary:salary,manager:manager");


SELECT department, count(*) FROM packtPubEmployee GROUP BY department;
```

Joining two DynamoDB tables

Sometimes we would also want to get the aggregate data from two DynamoDB tables; in that case, you create two Hive tables, which would be mapped to the corresponding tables in DynamoDB. Then you use the JOIN keyword and the key on which the tables should be joined to get the joined dataset.

```
CREATE EXTERNAL TABLE packtPubEmployee (empid String, yoj String,
department String, salary bigint, manager String)

STORED BY 'org.apache.hadoop.hive.dynamodb.DynamoDBStorageHandler'

TBLPROPERTIES ("dynamodb.table.name" = "Employee",

"dynamodb.column.mapping" =
"empid:empId,yoj:yoj,department:dept,salary:salary,manager:manager");
```

```
CREATE EXTERNAL TABLE packtPubDepartment (department String, name String,
head String)
STORED BY 'org.apache.hadoop.hive.dynamodb.DynamoDBStorageHandler'
TBLPROPERTIES ("dynamodb.table.name" = "Department",
"dynamodb.column.mapping" = "department:dept,name:name,head:head");


SELECT e.empid , d.name FROM
packtPubEmployee e JOIN packtPubDepartment d
ON (e.department = d.department);
```

This would result in a dataset that would have two columns: the first would be employee ID and second would be the department it belongs to. You can add more filtering using where conditions in case you need more specific information.

Joining tables from DynamoDB and S3

We also join tables from different sources, for example, one table from DynamoDB and another from AWS S3 stored as flat file, or a table from DynamoDB and a table created out of data present on HDFS. For such cases, you just need to create a table on Hive which would map to the correct location and correct service and then you can simply run the join table query. By the following commands, we would try to join a table from DynamoDB to a set of flat file present on AWS S3:

```
-- A DynamoDB table
CREATE EXTERNAL TABLE packtPubEmployee (empid String, yoj String,
department String, salary bigint, ,manager String)
STORED BY 'org.apache.hadoop.hive.dynamodb.DynamoDBStorageHandler'
TBLPROPERTIES ("dynamodb.table.name" = "Employee",
"dynamodb.column.mapping" =
"empid:empId,yoj:yoj,department:dept,salary:salary,manager:manager");


-- A table created from S3 flat files
CREATE EXTERNAL TABLE packtPubDepartment (department String, name String,
head String)
ROW FORMAT DELIMITED FIELDS TERMINATED BY ','
LOCATION 's3://bucket/path/';


-- Join the tables
SELECT e.empid , d.name FROM
packtPubEmployee e JOIN packtPubDepartment d
ON (e.department = d.department);
```

Again the output would be employee ID with its corresponding department name.

Importing data into DynamoDB

Sometimes there might be a use case where you need to move your application from some database to DynamoDB. In that case, you use the following techniques to get your data up on DynamoDB.

Importing data from AWS S3

Here again, we need to use EMR and Hive to create external tables and import the data from S3. First, we need to create a table in Hive that is mapped to a bucket on Amazon S3. Then, we need to create one more table that would be mapped to a table in DynamoDB, in which we need to dump this data. And then we can simply run insert into query to import data to DynamoDB from S3. The following code shows how to import data from the `packt-pub-employee` bucket to the `Employee` table in DynamoDB:

```
CREATE EXTERNAL TABLE packtPubEmployee_s3 (empid String, yoj String,
department String, salary bigint, manager String)
ROW FORMAT DELIMITED FIELDS TERMINATED BY ','
LOCATION 's3://packt-pub-employee/employee/';


CREATE EXTERNAL TABLE packtPubEmployee (empid String, yoj String,
department String, salary bigint, ,manager String)
STORED BY 'org.apache.hadoop.hive.dynamodb.DynamoDBStorageHandler'
TBLPROPERTIES ("dynamodb.table.name" = "Employee",
"dynamodb.column.mapping" =
"empid:empId,yoj:yoj,department:dept,salary:salary,manager:manager");


INSERT OVERWRITE TABLE packtPubEmployee SELECT * FROM packtPubEmployee_
s3;
```

You can also import data from S3 without specifying the attribute mapping as shown:

```
CREATE EXTERNAL TABLE packtPubEmployee_s3 (item map<string, string>)
ROW FORMAT DELIMITED FIELDS TERMINATED BY ','
LOCATION 's3://packt-pub-employee/employee/';


CREATE EXTERNAL TABLE packtPubEmployee (item map<string, string>)
STORED BY 'org.apache.hadoop.hive.dynamodb.DynamoDBStorageHandler'
TBLPROPERTIES ("dynamodb.table.name" = "Employee");


INSERT OVERWRITE TABLE packtPubEmployee SELECT * FROM packtPubEmployee_s3;
```

Here, instead of specifying attributes in the table, we are giving a single-map variable that would store all the values, and which would add the data to corresponding attributes. But as we don't have any attributes specified, we cannot query such tables in Hive as we would not have attribute names with us.

Importing data from HDFS

We saw data export to HDFS from DynamoDB; in the same manner, you can import data to DynamoDB from HDFS flat files. Here, first we need to create a table in hive that is linked to a directory on HDFS. Then, we need to create another table that links to a table in DynamoDB where you need to put the data. Now, you can simply insert data from the first to the second table, and you would be able to see the data imported in the DynamoDB table.

In the following example, we would try to import the data present on the HDFS path `/data/employee` to the `Employee` table in DynamoDB:

```
CREATE EXTERNAL TABLE packtPubEmployee_hdfs(empid String, yoj String,
department String, salary bigint, ,manager String)

ROW FORMAT DELIMITED FIELDS TERMINATED BY ','

LOCATION 'hdfs:///data/employee/';


CREATE EXTERNAL TABLE packtPubEmployee (empid String, yoj String,
department String, salary bigint, manager String)

STORED BY 'org.apache.hadoop.hive.dynamodb.DynamoDBStorageHandler'

TBLPROPERTIES ("dynamodb.table.name" = "Employee",

"dynamodb.column.mapping" =
"empid:empId,yoj:yoj,department:dept,salary:salary,manager:manager");


INSERT OVERWRITE TABLE packtPubEmployee SELECT * FROM packtPubEmployee_
hdfs;
```

Performance considerations while using EMR with DynamoDB

When we use EMR for data import/export, it consumes the provisioned throughput of the tables. It is like just another DynamoDB client. It is easy to measure the time required to import or export a certain amount of data from/to DynamoDB if you know the data size, and the read and write capacity units provisioned to the table. For example, the `Employee` table from DynamoDB needs to be exported to S3.

The size of the table is 10 GB and the read capacity provisioned in 50 units. The time required for the export, calculated as the time taken by EMR for 10 GB data export, will be 1073741824 bytes (10 GB) / 204800 bytes (50 Read Units) = 14.56 hours.

To reduce the time, we need to increase the read capacity units provisioned to the table. The following are some important things one should keep in mind in order to get the best out of DynamoDB and EMR integration.

- By default, EMR decides on its own the rate at which data should be fetched. It decides the read rate depending upon the capacity units provisioned for the table. But in case you are getting a high number of provisioned throughput exceeded information, you can set the read rate by setting a parameter `dynamodb.throughput.read.percent`. The range for this parameter is from 0.1 to 1.5. The default read rate is 0.5, which means that Hive will consume half of the capacity units provisioned to the table. You can increase the value if you need to increase the performance, but make sure that you keep watching the table's consumed capacity units and throttled request metrics and adjust the provisioned throughput.

  The parameter can be set on Hive console before you execute the query as follows:

  ```
  SET dynamodb.throughput.read.percent = 1.0
  ```

- Similar to that, we also set the write rate if we want to control the import to DynamoDB table. Here, we need the parameter `dynamodb.throughput.write.percent` the range of which varies from 0.1 to 1.5. Also, we need to set this before we run the query in the Hive console. Have a look at the following commands:

  ```
  SET dynamodb.throughput.write.percent = 1.2
  ```

- In the event of failures, Amazon retries the Hive queries. The default retry timeout is 2 minutes, but you can change it using parameter `dynamodb.retry.duration`. You need to mention the number of minutes after which Amazon should retry the query in case of no response as follows:

  ```
  SET dynamodb.retry.duration = 5;
  ```

  This would set the retry interval to 5 minutes.

- You can also improve the import/export performance by increasing the number of mappers. The number of mappers for a certain Hadoop cluster is dependent on the capacity of the hardware the cluster is using. Either you can increase the hardware configuration of the nodes or you can increase the number of nodes. Make a note that to do this, you need to stop the EMR cluster and make changes into it. There is one parameter, which you can also set to increase the number of mappers `mapred.tasktracker.map.tasks.maximum` that you set, to increase the performance. The only issue with increasing the value of this parameter is that it may cause out-of-memory issues for the nodes present in the EMR cluster. As this attribute is very specific to EMR-related operations, this cannot be simply set to Hive console. For this, you need to set it as a bootstrap action. More information about bootstrap actions is available at `http://docs.aws.amazon.com/ElasticMapReduce/latest/DeveloperGuide/emr-plan-bootstrap.html`.

Integrating with AWS Redshift

As I keep on saying, this is a data era and every piece of data keeps on telling us something. Acting on this need, Amazon has introduced Redshift, which is a data warehouse as a service that allows you to dump your data on cloud with minimum cost. Redshift has power query language that allows us to drill TBs and PBs of data in seconds. It helps users to analyze data cheaper and faster.

Now, you must be wondering how this tool could help someone who has his application database as DynamoDB. Well, the answer is quite simple, most of the organization tries to keep their application database size easily controllable. This means that they tend to purge or archive old/stale data periodically. In such cases, it is good to have a data warehousing solution in cloud itself. So, you can keep your application live data on DynamoDB and use Redshift to dump old data to archive and analyze.

Unlike DynamoDB, Redshift is a SQL-based data warehousing tool. It comes with a powerful SQL query tool, which is giving tough competition to other tools, such as Hive, Impala, Google Big Query, and Apache Drill. We can simply copy data present on DynamoDB to Redshift and start using it for Business intelligence applications.

Even though both DynamoDB and Redshift are from Amazon, we need to take care of a few things as these two tools are meant to do two different things. The following are a few important things one should consider before using Redshift with DynamoDB:

- DynamoDB is schema-less, but Redshift needs pre-defined schema to store data in an appropriate manner.

- We don't have any null value concept in DynamoDB, so we need to specify how Redshift should handle attributes with null or empty values.

  For example, suppose in an `Employee` table, we have one item {empid:123, name:XYZ} and another one {empid:111,name:PQR, post:CEO}. Here, when we copy this data to Redshift, we have to specify schema such as {empid, name, post} when creating a table. Also, we need to specify how Redshift would handle the value for post attribute for the first item.

- Also, DynamoDB table names can be up to 255 characters and can contain dot(.) and dash(-), whereas Redshift table names can be up to 127 characters only, and it does not allow dot(.) or dash(-) in any table name.

- The most important thing to note is that the DynamoDB data type does not directly connect to Redshift data types. So, we need to take care that the data types and sizes of columns are appropriate.

Now, we will see how to perform actual integration with Redshift.

Exporting data from DynamoDB

When integrating with Redshift, we have to simply copy data from a DynamoDB table to a Redshift table. Unlike in EMR, we need a connection from DynamoDB to Redshift at the time of data copy only. There are advantages as well as disadvantages with this approach. The good thing is that once the copying is done, Redshift processes would not use any DynamoDB provisioned throughput, and a not-so-good thing is that we have to keep two copies of data one on DynamoDB and another one on Redshift.

Amazon Redshift has a powerful COPY command that can fetch data from DynamoDB tables faster using **massive parallel processing** (**MPP**). MPP allows Redshift processes to distribute the load and fetch data in parallel and in a faster manner. One thing we have to note over here is the COPY command leverages provisioned throughput of the DynamoDB table, so we have to make sure enough throughput is provisioned in order to avoid provisioned throughput exceeded exception.

 It is recommended not to use production DynamoDB tables to directly copy data to Redshift. As I had mentioned earlier, Redshift's MPP may drain out all the read provisioned throughput, and if there are any important requests coming to the DynamoDB table from production, then it may cause some disturbance to the application. To avoid this, either you can create a duplicate table in DynamoDB, which is copy of the original table, and then use the COPY command on this table, or you can limit the READRATIO parameter to use only limited resources.

READRATIO is a parameter in the COPY command that sets how much Redshift should use from DynamoDB's provisioned throughput. If you want Redshift to utilize full provisioned throughput from the DynamoDB table, then you can set the value of this parameter to 100.

The COPY command works in the following manner:

- First, it matches the attributes in the DynamoDB table with columns in the Redshift table.
- The Redshift table matches the DynamoDB attributes in a sensitive manner.
- The columns in Redshift that do not match to any attribute in DynamoDB are set as NULL or empty, depending on the value specified in EMPTYASNULL option in the COPY command.
- Currently, DynamoDB columns with only scalar data types are supported, that is, columns with data types in string and number are only supported. Data types SET and BINARY are not supported.
- The attributes from DynamoDB that are not present in the Redshift table are simply ignored.

Suppose you want to export the Employee table from DynamoDB to Redshift, then you can simply use the following syntax:

```
COPY Employee_RS FROM 'dynamodb://Employee'
CREDENTIALS 'aws_access_key_id=<your-access-key>;aws_secret_access_
key=<your-secret-key>'
```

In the case of readratio 50, the first line mentions the name of the tables in Redshift and DynamoDB. The second line is to provide credentials, that is, access key and secret key. In the third line, you need to mention how much provisioned throughput Redshift should use from DynamoDB table. Here, I have mentioned 50 which means 50 percent of the table's provisioned read capacity units would be used.

Alternatively, you can also create temporary credentials and access keys and use it for the purpose of copying data. The benefit of using temporary credentials is that first, they are temporary, and second, they can be used only once and expire after a certain time. But one needs to be sure that the temporary credentials are valid for the entire time frame of the copy task.

The following is the syntax to use temporary credentials:

```
copy Employee_RS from 'dynamodb://Employee'
credentials 'aws_access_key_id=<temporary-access-key>;aws_secret_access_
key=<temporary-secret-key>;token=<temporary-token>'
readratio 50;
```

Automatic compression and sampling

Sometimes you would be wondering that the COPY command has used more than the required provisioned throughput for data load. So, the answer for that is that the COPY command by default applies some compression on data being loaded to Redshift. To do so, it first samples a certain number of rows and then see if it works fine. Once done, all these rows are discarded. The number of rows to sample is decided by the parameter COMPROWS the default value of which is 10000 rows.

 If your data contains multibyte characters (Mandarin (Chinese) characters), then you should use VARCHAR columns in Redshift tables to load data. VARCHAR supports 4-byte UTF-8 characters. The CHAR data type supports only single-byte characters. You cannot load data comprising more than 4-byte characters.

You can get more details about the COPY command at http://docs.aws.amazon. com/redshift/latest/dg/r_COPY.html and http://docs.aws.amazon.com/ redshift/latest/dg/r_COPY_command_examples.html.

With Redshift being the data warehouse, the majority of the time, there would be a use case of only exporting data from DynamoDB to Redshift, and in a very rare situation someone would think of importing data back from Redshift to DynamoDB, hence there is no such best method available till date.

Integrating with AWS CloudSearch

Amazon CloudSearch is a search engine as a service from Amazon that allows users to store their documents on CloudSearch, provides indexing on those documents and provides a search engine kind of functionality with faceted search options. CloudSearch scales as the number of documents increases with time. Using CloudSearch is quite easy — you just need to create one CloudSearch domain where you need to specify the attributes of each document you are going to store. Appropriate data types are provided in order to improve the search functionality.

To store a document in CloudSearch, you have to generate your data in SDF format. SDF is nothing but Search Document Format, which is a JSON document that holds the metadata about the document with actual data. Once the document is stored on CloudSearch, you can simply search for the document using the CloudSearch console or search API given by Amazon.

There might be a use case where you want to use DynamoDB as your storage tool, and you want to implement a use case where end users need to search from a range of items. In this case, if the search functionality is a primary requirement, then you should use DynamoDB for storage and CloudSearch for search functionality. You can use DynamoDB as primary data storage unit and keep a copy of this data on CloudSearch to deal with faster-searching requirements. Consider an example of a bookstore application where users will look to search for books online with book name, author name, year of publishing, and so on. For such kind of use case, CloudSearch is the best fit.

In order to use CloudSearch with DynamoDB, perform the following steps:

1. Configure CloudSearch domain
2. Export data from DynamoDB to CloudSearch

Configuring CloudSearch domain

To match with DynamoDB table attributes, there is an easy way to configure the CloudSearch domain. The following is a stepwise tutorial to do the same.

Using AWS management console

Now we will go through instructions on how to use the AWS management console:

1. Sign in to AWS CloudSearch console at `https://console.aws.amazon.com/cloudsearch/` and you will get the following screenshot:

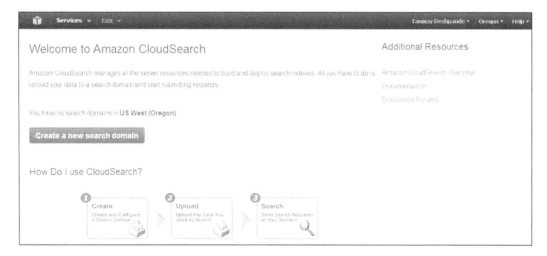

2. Then click on **Create a new search domain** option, and you will see a new window popping up asking for the details as shown in the following screenshot. Upon giving the proper domain name, you can click on the **Continue** button.

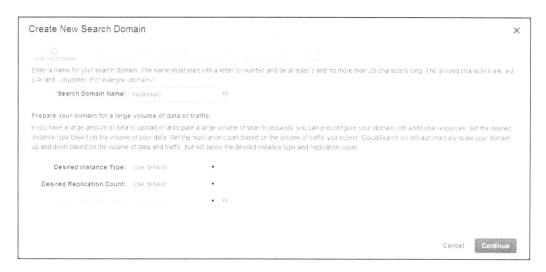

3. In the next screen, it will ask for index configurations. Here we want to create a search domain for one of our tables in DynamoDB, so you can select **Analyze sample item(s) from Amazon DynamoDB**. Then it will load a list of DynamoDB tables associated with the given account. Here I am selecting a table called **Book**. It will also ask for read capacity units, which is a value CloudSearch would use when reading data from DynamoDB for sampling purposes. You can click on **Continue** to proceed with data sampling.

4. Depending upon the type of data present in a given table, Amazon will recommend the index configuration as shown in the following screenshot. You can modify the configuration if required. And click on **Continue** to create the domain.

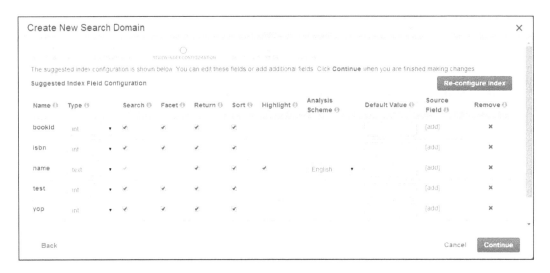

Once the domain creation is done, half of the things are done. This configuration is just for index creation, and this does not mean there is a sync between DynamoDB and CloudSearch domain now. We still need to populate the documents by any of the given methods.

Using command-line tools

We can do whatever we did using the management console using command-line tools. This includes the following two steps:

1. We have to generate the sample search document format from a DynamoDB table and store it on the local disk or S3 bucket. The syntax is as follows:

    ```
    cs-import-documents --source ddb://Book --output c:\samples\book
    ```

    This will generate sample SDF documents using internal API and will dump those on your local disk.

2. The next thing that we need to do is configure an index using these newly generated SDFs that you have stored on your local disk:

```
cs-configure-from-sdf --domain mydomain --source c:\ samples\book\*
```

Once done, you will see that the index configuration is done for the CloudSearch domain.

Export data from DynamoDB to CloudSearch

To upload data from DynamoDB to CloudSearch, you can use the CloudSearch management console, or you can use the command-line tool.

Using AWS management console

In this section, we will see how to export data from DynamoDB to CloudSearch using the AWS management console:

1. Sign in to the AWS CloudSearch console `https://console.aws.amazon.com/cloudsearch/` and you will see a list of CloudSearch domains you have created already. You can select the appropriate one to move ahead, as shown in the following screenshot:

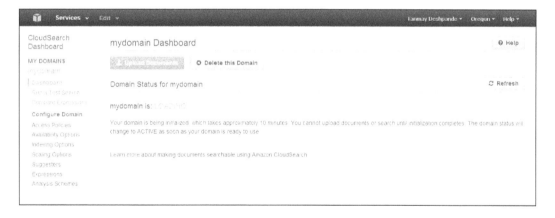

Make a note that it takes some time to get your CloudSearch domain active; till then, you have to wait.

2. On clicking **Upload Documents**, you would see a new pop up on your window asking for details. Here, you can select the **Item(s) from Amazon DynamoDB** option and can select the table from which you need to upload the data. You can also mention how much of the of read capacity units it should use (in percentage terms) to fetch the data. You can click on **Continue** to move ahead. Have a look at the following screenshot:

3. Internally, it will convert the data into SDF, and once done, you can click on **Upload Documents** to start uploading the data, as shown in the following screenshot.

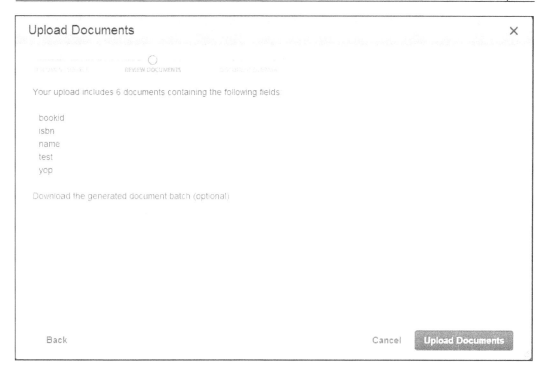

A sample batch of SDF documents would look as follows:

```
[ {
  "type" : "add",
  "id" : "1008_1009",
  "fields" : {
    "bookid" : "1008",
    "test" : "766",
    "isbn" : "111",
    "name" : "Mastering DynamoDB",
    "yop" : "1009"
  }
}, {
  "type" : "add",
  "id" : "1008_2000",
  "fields" : {
    "bookid" : "1008",
    "yop" : "2000"
  }
```

```
}, {
  "type" : "add",
  "id" : "1008_2009",
  "fields" : {
    "bookid" : "1008",
    "test" : "111",
    "isbn" : "1111",
    "yop" : "2009"
  }
}]
```

Using command line tools

To upload the data from DynamoDB to CloudSearch, we need to run the `cs-import-documents` command in the following manner:

```
cs-import-documents --domain mydomain --source ddb://Book
```

Here, we are uploading documents to the `mydomain` CloudSearch domain from the DynamoDB table called `Book`.

 Make a note that when we keep data at two sources, it is always challenging to maintain them in sync. When we create the CloudSearch domain from the DynamoDB table, we just borrow information to create the index and nothing else. So once the document upload is done, for any update or delete, there should be a similar operation performed on CloudSearch with each DynamoDB data change. You can programmatically do that by writing code for both DynamoDB and CloudSearch updates one after another. This would help in keeping your system up-to-date.

Summary

In this chapter, we talked about using the AWS ecosystem to develop and deploy your application on cloud. We started with AWS EMR integration with DynamoDB. We also used AWS S3 as the staging environment for the integration. By creating the Hive table using EMR, we also learned to query data in DynamoDB. This integration helped us to give data analytics solution for your application. So that we don't need to go anywhere else, simply keep your application database as DynamoDB and integrate with EMR to get better insights from your data.

In the next section, we discussed how to integrate DynamoDB with AWS Redshift, which is a data warehousing solution from Amazon. So if you need to stage out your data for Business Intelligence applications, you can simply store it on Redshift.

In the last section, we talked about how to make your data searchable using the CloudSearch engine. We saw how to create the CloudSearch domain from DynamoDB tables and also used command-line options to configure the index for a given table. After that, we explored options on uploading data from DynamoDB to CloudSearch.

I am sure that after reading this chapter you can see your end-to-end application running on AWS Cloud without any overhead of maintaining so many systems.

In the next chapter, we are going to study a couple of use cases that are already implemented, and we will try to understand what we could do if we need to build something similar to these systems.

7
DynamoDB – Use Cases

Now we have seen all the core and important parts of DynamoDB. Now you must know what DynamoDB is, what the data model for it is, how DynamoDB actually works, what the best practices are, how to impose security, access controls on tables, and so on. In the previous chapter, we talked about integrating DynamoDB with various AWS components, such as S3, Redshift, EMR, and so on. Now I am sure you must have started thinking in terms of how to build an application using DynamoDB and what steps are involved in it. So in this chapter, we are going to see a couple of use cases that should give you an idea of what it takes to use DynamoDB as your application database.

In this chapter, we will consider the following two use cases:

- A bookstore application
- A knowledge market website (For example, Stack Overflow or Yahoo Answers)

Bookstore application

A bookstore application consists of a web portal where we will sell books online. This web application would allow users to search for books by name or the author's name, select and purchase books as per their choice, and pay for the books. This bookstore allows users to sign in using their Facebook, Google, and Amazon accounts.

Technology stack

Now that we have defined the problem statement, we will have to select the technology stack in order to go ahead with it. The following is the technology stack:

- Programming language: Java
- Database: DynamoDB
- Search engine: AWS CloudSearch
- Web server: Tomcat. This can be hosted on the AWS EC2 instance
- Analytics: AWS EMR

Architecture

As we do in any software development life cycle, let's try to build the architecture diagram as follows for better understanding:

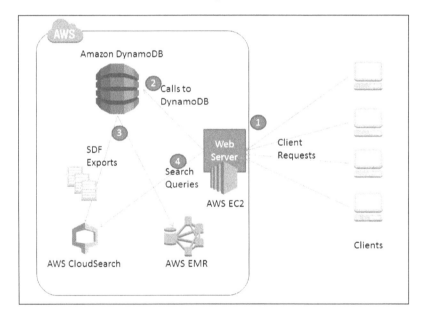

The previous diagram shows how we can connect different AWS and non-AWS components together. We will also use AWS **Secure Token Service** (**STS**), which we have seen in *Chapter 5*, *Advanced Topics*, in order to authenticate the users.

The flow for this application would be as follows:

1. A user logs in to the application using their Facebook, Google, or Amazon credentials.

2. AWS sends this request to identity providers for verification; in return, it will get the identity token. Using this token, the client sends this request to STS to get temporary credentials.

3. Now the web server acts on behalf of the client and makes requests to DynamoDB. If the user has the required privileges, then DynamoDB gives back the required data. For example, here we can consider the action of adding new books to a book table by the admin user.

4. There can be requests coming from various other users to know more about a certain book, for example, the price of a book, reviews of a book, and so on.

5. We should also write code for adding book metadata to CloudSearch. We can have a background process that adds this data to CloudSearch from DynamoDB, or we can simply call the CloudSearch API from our code whenever we make an entry into DynamoDB.

6. We can write AWS EMR import queries to fetch the data from DynamoDB to the EMR cluster or AWS S3 for analytics, for example, trending books, trending queries, recommendation engine based on user search history, and so on.

As our focus for this book is DynamoDB, let's try to put down some information on what the tables could be and what their schema would be.

DynamoDB data model

Depending upon the features that we want to support, I have listed down the following tables with their primary keys.

Table Name	Primary key type	Hash key	Range key
Book (yop,bkId,..)	Hash and range	**Yop (Year of Publishing)**: This will allow us to retrieve books as per the year in which they got published	bkId – unique book ID
Author (authId,..)	Hash key	authId – unique author ID	NA
Publisher (pubId,..)	Hash key	pubId – unique publisher ID	NA

Here, you will observe that we are using short names such as bkId instead of bookId or yop instead of YearOfPublishing, as we have learned in *Chapter 4, Best Practices*, that even the attribute name size is being counted while calculating an item. So it is very important to have all these things in mind before doing the schema design.

Here, while storing the book data, we are using a unique book ID as hash key and year of publication as range key. It is always important to have a good choice of hash and range keys that distributes the load to multiple nodes in the cluster. This helps performance improvement.

Sample data for the tables would be like the content of the following screenshot:

```
Book (yop, bokId,..)

{
        "yop": "2014",
        "bkId": "100",
        "title": "Mastering DynamoDB",
        "authors": ["Tanmay Deshpande"],
        "ISBN" :"222-222-22222",
        "chapters": 9
}

{
        "yop": "2013",
        "bkId": "200",
        "title": "Mastering RedShift",
        "authors": ["XYZ"],
        "ISBN" :"222-222-28888",
        "chapters": 10
}
```

You can also create secondary indexes on attributes such as title and authors in order to enable use cases like getting book data by title or getting books for a given author.

It is also important to have an association between the tables in order to get linked information. We have already seen relationship modeling in *Chapter 2, Data Models*.

Implementation

Once the data modeling is finalized, you can start with actual implementation. For that you can start with creating tables in DynamoDB. You can use the AWS console to create the tables, or you can simply use the SDK and enter a create table request; for example, you can use Java/PHP/.NET APIs to create the table, update the table, delete the table, and so on. We have already seen the syntax to do this in various languages in *Chapter 2, Data Models*.

You can simply pick up the use cases one by one and start writing APIs. You can write code to add new books to the table, delete certain books, update the book data, and so on. You can simultaneously keep testing your code for incremental development.

Integration with other AWS components

As we have discussed earlier, we will use AWS CloudSearch to give search functionality to the user. We can create a domain for the same as we have learned in *Chapter 6, Integrating DynamoDB with Other AWS Components*. We can use auto index generation options provided by the AWS CloudSearch console to get seamless integration. As seen earlier, for already existing data in DynamoDB, we can use the CloudSearch console tool to upload the data, and for each new entry, you can write a CloudSearch API call to upload the book data in SDF format to CloudSearch.

You can also integrate a query API from CloudSearch to help users search in the book database. For more details, check out the CloudSearch API documentation at `http://aws.amazon.com/documentation/cloudsearch/`.

In the architecture diagram, we have also shown that we can use AWS EMR to process batch jobs to get more information about the data stored. We can go ahead and implement a rating/review system for the books and authors and can also implement a recommendation engine that recommends books to users as per their likes.

Deployment

Depending on the programming language selection, deployment scenarios would be varied. Suppose we have implemented the code in Java, then we can use the Apache Tomcat server for deployment of our application. We can use the EC2 instance to install Tomcat and deploy the application on it. To make that application scalable, you can use AWS Elastic Load Balancing.

Knowledge market website

A knowledge market website is a place where users can post questions to the community and look for answers. A question can be a part of one or more topics that can also be subscribed to by the individual users. A good example of such a website is www.StackOverflow.com, which many of us might already be using. Let's try to follow the same approach we did for our first use case.

Technology stack

The technology stack for this application is much the same as the previous one, except a few. Have a look at the following list:

- Programming language: Java (you can choose your preferred language)
- Database: DynamoDB
- Web server: Tomcat (Tomcat can be hosted on the AWS EC2 instance)
- Data Archiving: AWS S3

We can add other AWS components like SNS to send notifications to users if they see any activity on the question they had asked or answered.

Architecture

Now we will try to draw the architecture diagram for this application:

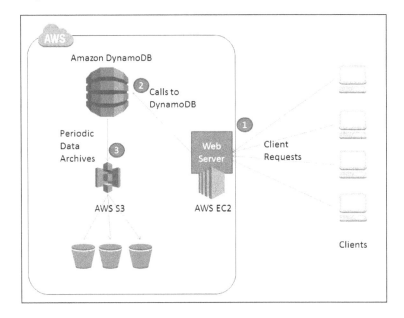

The previous diagram shows how the overall application functionality would look. The working of the application is explained in the following points:

- The clients sends requests to the application deployed on Tomcat or any other server.

- The code written for the application connects with DynamoDB to perform the operation. Sample operations would include adding a new question, adding a reply to an already existing question, deleting a topic/question, and so on.

- AWS S3 can be used to archive the data from DynamoDB; we have seen how to archive data on S3 using EMR in *Chapter 6, Integrating DynamoDB with Other AWS Components.*

- Like the previous example, we would also be using the web identity federation provided by AWS STS in order to maintain the session management. Read *Chapter 5, Advanced Topics*, for more detail.

DynamoDB data model

Depending upon the features we want to support, I have listed down the following tables with their primary keys:

Table name	Primary key type	Hash key	Range key
Topic (Name, ...)	Hash key	Name	NA
Question (TopicName, Question,..)	Hash and range keys	TopicName	Question
Answer(Id, AnswerTs)	Hash and range key	Answer Id	Answer timestamp
Votes(AnswerId, ..)	Hash key	Answer Id	

The previous table gives the kind of data we want to store and retrieve for the users. Here, the Topic table would contain all the topics we have in our application. Here, we have only the hash key for this table. The Question table would have both hash and range keys, that is, TopicName and Question, respectively. Here we can save information for questions like the description, the identity of the one who has added that question, and so on.

The Answer table stores the information about the answers given by users. Here, we have the timestamp at which the user has added the answer as the range key. Keeping the timestamp as the range helps equal data distribution across the cluster.

Finally, we have also kept one table that lists the votes one has gathered for the answers given. Sample data for the given tables would look like the following tables:

Topic table

```
{
   "name": "Cloud Computing",
   "createdAt": "23-06-2011T13: 00: 05Z",
   "description": "This topic is for all Cloud Computing related
questions."
   "subscribers" : 24455
}

{
   "name": "Big Data",
   "createdAt": "23-07-2011T13: 00: 05Z",
   "description": "This topic is for all Big Data related
questions."
   "subscribers" : 55886
}

{
   "name": "NoSQL",
   "createdAt": "26-06-2011T13: 00: 05Z",
   "description": "This topic is for all NoSQL related questions."
   "subscribers" : 2765
}
```

Questions Tables

```
{
   "topicName": "Cloud Computing",
   "question" : "What is Cloud Computing"
   "createdAt": "23-06-2011T13: 00: 05Z",
   "askedBy" : "abc"
}
```

Questions Tables

```
{
   "topicName": "Big Data",
   "question" : "What is Big Data"
   "createdAt": "23-06-2012T13: 00: 05Z",
   "askedBy" : "xyz"
}
```

Answers

```
{
   "id" : "Big Data#What is Big Data"
   "ts": "23-06-2011T13: 00: 05Z",
   "postedby": "XYZ",
   "message" : "huge data"
}


{
   "id" : "Cloud Computing#What is Cloud Computing"
   "ts": "23-06-2011T13: 00: 05Z",
   "postedby": "XYZ",
   "message" : "Using network, storage etc as service"
}
```

Votes

```
{
   "answerId" : "Cloud Computing#What is Cloud Computing#23-06-
2011T13:00:05Z",
   "ups" : 2344
   "downs" : 2
}


{
   "answerId" : "Cloud Computing#Why is Cloud Computing#23-06-
2011T13:00:05Z",
   "ups" : 23
   "downs" : 288
}
```

Here, you would have observed that we are using the ID columns to uniquely identify the item.

Implementation

Once the data modeling is finalized, you can start with actual implementation. For that, you can start with creating tables in DynamoDB. You can use the AWS console to create the tables, or you can simply use the SDK and enter a create table request. For example, you can use Java/PHP/.NET APIs to create tables, update tables, delete tables, and so on. We have already seen the syntax to do the same in various languages in *Chapter 2, Data Models*.

You can simply pick up the use cases one by one and start writing APIs. You can take the reference of the code snippets we have seen in *Chapter 2, Data Models*, for further detail.

Integration with other AWS components

As we have shown in the architecture diagram, we will also build a background job that would periodically archive data, AWS S3. We can keep some buckets handy in order to archive the data. To give an example, let's assume we want to archive data present in the Questions and Answers tables to a bucket called QnA-backup on AWS S3. Then, you can execute the following query on AWS EMR:

```
CREATE EXTERNAL TABLE Questions_2012 (topicName string, question string,
createdAt, postedBy)
STORED BY 'org.apache.hadoop.hive.dynamodb.DynamoDBStorageHandler'
TBLPROPERTIES ("dynamodb.table.name" = "Questions",
"dynamodb.column.mapping" = "topicName:topicName, question:question,creat
eAt:createdAt, postedby:postedBy");
```

Once the one-to-one mapping is done, we can execute INSERT into the command to export the S3:

```
INSERT OVERWRITE DIRECTORY 's3:// QnA-backup /questions/' SELECT *
FROM Questions_2012;
```

For more details, you can refer to *Chapter 6, Integrating DynamoDB with other AWS Components*.

Deployment

Depending on the programming language selection, deployment scenarios would be varied. Suppose we have implemented the code in Java, then we can use the Apache Tomcat server for deployment of our application. We can use the EC2 instance to install Tomcat and deploy the application on it. To make that application scalable, you can use AWS Elastic Load Balancing.

You can read more about real-time case studies where DynamoDB is used at `http://aws.amazon.com/solutions/case-studies/`.

Summary

In this chapter, we talked about two sample use cases in which DynamoDB is being used as an application database. The purpose of this chapter was to give an idea to the readers about what approach one should follow in order to get DynamoDB into production. It is advised that one should try to understand the application development process and get started with actual application building.

Here, I have also tried to show how we can integrate various AWS services in order to have our complete application running on Cloud itself. The motive is to just give the idea and show the complete picture to you all; it would be great if you follow the referenced chapters thoroughly for implementation details.

In the next chapter, we are going to see various useful tools from AWS and third-party contributors. These tools are helpful for any DynamoDB developers and can be used/reused easily.

8
Useful Libraries and Tools

In the last chapter, we discussed a couple of sample use cases where we explained the flow of implementing an application using DynamoDB as a database. We also discussed how we integrate other AWS services and make the best use of the AWS ecosystem. In this chapter, our focus is going to be on some useful tools and libraries available for our use. Some of the tools and libraries are given by AWS to help their customers, while many others have been contributed by open source developers for the benefit of the community.

We have plenty of interesting tools and libraries available that are related to DynamoDB. In this chapter, we are going to explore some of them and their usage.

Libraries

There are various libraries available for general use in DynamoDB. Most of these libraries are community contributed and are maintained by individual users. We are going to start with a couple of interesting libraries made available by Amazon itself. After that, we will also try to list down available community-contributed and language-specific libraries.

Transaction library

The Transaction library has been built on top of the AWS SDK for Java and is only available for Java-based applications. This client library has been provided in order to reduce the development efforts one has to put in to support atomic operations. For those who are not aware of what a transaction means, consider an example where you need to perform two to three operations one after another and commit them only when all the operations are successful. If any of the operations fails in between, the complete process should be failed, reverting all the operations before the failed operation.

The Transaction library supports atomic writes and isolated reads. Let's try to understand these one by one. It would not be an exaggeration if I were to say this library brings DynamoDB to completion by supporting atomicity, consistency , isolation, and durability (ACID properties) with regards to multiple items.

Atomic writes

A good example of a transaction is online money transfer from one bank account to another bank account. It consists of various stages that are as follows:

- Initiating money transfer from bank account A
- Deducting money from bank account A
- Getting interbank money transfer clearance
- Depositing money to bank account B
- Notifying both account holders about the transaction

Here, it is very important that the set of instructions gets completed. Suppose any one operation fails, then all previous operations should be reverted to their original state. The operations should fail or succeed as a unit. If this does not happen, then the system would be in the wrong state.

In order to solve this problem, Amazon has given us the Transaction library, which helps perform atomic operations. The library is quite easy to use. It needs two DynamoDB tables with minimal read and writes provisioned capacity units that keep track of the operations within a transaction. The first table stores the transaction, while the second one stores the pretransaction image of items involved in that transaction.

1. To begin with, you need to first create an Amazon DynamoDB client. You also need to have two tables created in your DynamoDB console to be used by the Transaction library.

2. The Transaction library is hosted on GitHub, so you can download the maven project from `https://github.com/awslabs/dynamodb-transactions`.

3. You can select the download zip option on the GitHub page, and it will download the source code. Once you have the source code, please build it using Maven by running the following command:

```
mvn clean install -Dgpg.skip=true
```

4. This will install the Transaction library in your `.m2` repository, and now you can start accessing its classes from Eclipse or any other IDE you are using.

So let's start with creating the DynamoDB client as we do for any other operations using the following command:

```
AmazonDynamoDBClient   client = new AmazonDynamoDBClient();
```

You can also set other details such as region, credentials, and so on. Now, it's time to create the DynamoDB tables we are going to use to save the transaction metadata. This can be done by calling `verifyOrCreateTransactionTable` and `verifyOrCreateTransactionImagesTable` as follows:

```
    TransactionManager.verifyOrCreateTransactionTable(client,
"Transaction", 10, 5, 30);
    TransactionManager. verifyOrCreateTransactionImagesTable (client,
"TransactionImages", 10, 5, 30);
```

The parameters contain the DynamoDB client, the name of the DynamoDB transaction table, read capacity units, write capacity units, and time to wait. This is a one-time activity and need not be performed more than once.

Now let's see how to create a transaction and execute it. To begin with, initialize the transaction manager, an implementation of which is provided by AWS, with names of the transaction and transaction images tables, as follows:

```
TransactionManager txm = new TransactionManager(client, "Transaction",
"Transaction_Images");
```

Now create a new transaction from the transaction manager and perform the operation you want to perform:

```
// Create new transaction from the transaction manager
Transaction tx = txm.newTransaction();
```

Suppose you need to deposit money from one account to another account, then you need to make `updateItem` requests, and if both are successful, only then should we commit the transaction. This can be done as shown in the following code. The following code deducts 100 units from account number 2001:

```
// Deduct money from account
// Create Hash Map of item with attributes to be updated.
Map<String, AttributeValueUpdate> updateItemsForDebit = new
HashMap<String, AttributeValueUpdate>();

// Hash key of item to be updated
HashMap<String, AttributeValue> primaryKeyForDebit = new
HashMap<String, AttributeValue>();
primaryKeyForDebit.put("accountNumber", new AttributeValue().
withN("2001"));
```

```
// Reduce the balance by 100
updateItemsForDebit.put("balance",
new  AttributeValueUpdate().withAction(AttributeAction.ADD)
        .withValue(new AttributeValue().withN("-100")));

UpdateItemRequest debitRequest = new UpdateItemRequest()
    .withTableName("Bank").withKey(primaryKey)
    .withReturnValues(ReturnValue.UPDATED_NEW)
    .withAttributeUpdates(updateItems);

// Execute the transaction
tx.updateItem(debitRequest);
```

Now we need to create a similar request that would add and increase the balance by 100 to account 2002, as follows:

```
// Add 100 to the balance to account
// Create Hash Map of item with attributes to be updated.
Map<String, AttributeValueUpdate> updateItemsForCredit = new
HashMap<String, AttributeValueUpdate>();



// Hash key of item to be updated
HashMap<String, AttributeValue> primaryKeyForCredit = new
HashMap<String, AttributeValue>();

primaryKeyForCredit.put("accountNumber", new AttributeValue().
withN("2002"));

// Add 100 to the exiting balance
updateItemsForCredit.put("balance",
      new AttributeValueUpdate()
.withAction(AttributeAction.ADD)
      .withValue(new AttributeValue()
.withN("100")));

UpdateItemRequest creditRequest = new UpdateItemRequest()
        .withTableName("Bank").withKey(primaryKey1)
        .withReturnValues(ReturnValue.UPDATED_NEW)
        .withAttributeUpdates(updateItems1);

// Execute the transaction

tx.updateItem(creditRequest);
```

At this time, we would have the values updated in the tables, but this is not yet committed. So let's commit the transaction using the following code:

```
tx.commit();
```

Once this statement is executed, only then do you see that the values are committed.

Isolated reads

The Transaction library supports three different levels of isolation as follows:

- Fully isolated
- Committed
- Uncommitted

Fully isolated reads lock the items during the transaction just as we obtain locks during writes. This means that whenever you execute a command to get an item with the fully isolated option, the transaction manager puts a lock on that item and returns the result to the client. Committed reads are like consistent reads. If the transaction detects a lock on an item, then it reads the old value of the item. Uncommitted reads are dirty reads. Executing a get-item request with the uncommitted option is the cheapest one, but they are very dangerous to use as, if the transaction fails, the data we read might get rolled back. So if your application use case is comfortable with such behavior, only then should you go ahead with this type of reads.

The following is an example of reading an item using a committed read:

```
// Key for the item to be read
HashMap<String, AttributeValue> primaryKey = new HashMap<String,
AttributeValue>();
primaryKey.put("accountNumber", new AttributeValue().withN("2002"));

// Invoke get item request from transaction manager

Map<String, AttributeValue> item = txm.getItem(new GetItemRequest()
.withKey(primaryKey)
.withTableName("Bank"),
IsolationLevel.COMMITTED).getItem();
```

More details on this library are available at https://github.com/awslabs/dynamodb-transactions/blob/master/DESIGN.md.

Geo library

Amazon has provided us with a library that can help you do geographic operations and use it in your applications; it's called Geo library. The most common use of Geo libraries happens for mobile applications. This library helps you build location-aware mobile applications.

This library can help you store a **Point of Interest** (**POI**). For example, you have decided to create an application that shows the fine-dining restaurants within a certain range of your current location. This library would first let you store some restaurants that are POIs for you. And then, you can query all restaurants within a 500 metre range of your current geographical location.

Let's get into the details of this use case to understand this library better. To get started, first you need to download the source of this library and do a maven build on it. You can download the source from GitHub at `https://github.com/awslabs/dynamodb-geo`.

You can either clone or directly download the Zip file from GitHub. Once you have the source code, you can build the jar by running the following Maven command:

```
mvn clean install -Dgpg.skip=true
```

Now, let's see how to use this library. To begin with, as usual, you need to create a DynamoDB client with credentials and other things. Once you have the client ready, you need to create a table, say, `geo-table` that you will be using to do all geography-related data storing. You need to give this table's name to `GeoDataManagerConfiguration` to create `GeoDataManager` as shown in the following code:

```
AmazonDynamoDBClient client = new AmazonDynamoDBClient();

// Set geo table in configuration
GeoDataManagerConfiguration geoDataManagerConfiguration = new
GeoDataManagerConfiguration(
        client, "geo-table");

// Create Geo data manager
GeoDataManager geoDataManager = new GeoDataManager(geoDataManagerConf
iguration);
```

Once you are ready with the geo data manager, you have to create geo points to save in the table, which can be retrieved later. A geo point is a data model created to store geographic points. It contains attributes such as latitude and longitude. You need to also give one unique ID for this geo point as the range key attribute. To store further information, you can keep on adding other attributes. Consider the following example:

```
// Set geo table in configuration
GeoDataManagerConfiguration geoDataManagerConfiguration = new
GeoDataManagerConfiguration(
        client, "geo-table");
// Create Geo data manager
GeoDataManager geoDataManager = new GeoDataManager(geoDataManagerConf
iguration);


// Create geo point
GeoPoint geoPoint = new GeoPoint(18.518229,73.85705);

// Create unique range key attribute
AttributeValue rangekey = new AttributeValue().withS("POI_000001");

// Create attribute for storing restaurant name
AttributeValue resName = new AttributeValue().withS("Hotel TAJ");

// Create put point request for storing data in dynamodb table
PutPointRequest request = new PutPointRequest(geoPoint, rangekey);

// Add attribute name
request.getPutItemRequest().getItem().put("name", resName);

// Invoke put point method
geoDataManager.putPoint(request);
```

You can keep on adding such items to increase your database and support for various cities. As shown in the previous example, you can also add additional attributes (in this case name). The library encodes this geo point into the GeoJSON format. You can read more about GeoJSON at http://geojson.org/.

Now that you have stored the restaurant data into DynamoDB, you can simply start querying that data using methods provided by the library.

Query rectangle

The Geo library allows us to find all geo points falling between a pair of geo points. This searches all the items which are part of the rectangle when drawn using the given geo points. By giving these kinds of input, you can run the query rectangle, which would give you back all items falling in that rectangle. The following is the syntax for this operation:

```
// Min geo point
GeoPoint minGeoPoint = new GeoPoint(18.514973, 73.850698);

// Max geo point
GeoPoint maxGeoPoint = new GeoPoint(18.522624, 73.864088);


// Create query rectangle request
QueryRectangleRequest rectangleRequest = new QueryRectangleRequest(
      minGeoPoint, maxGeoPoint);

// Invoke query rectangle method
QueryRectangleResult rectangleResult = geoDataManager
      .queryRectangle(rectangleRequest);

// Get items from the result
for (Map<String, AttributeValue> item : rectangleResult.getItem()) {
   System.out.println("Item :" + item);
}
```

This would result in listing all items inside that rectangle.

Query radius

Similar to what we saw in the *Query rectangle* section. Amazon gives us an API that can list all items present in the radius of a certain circle drawn from a given geo point. Here, the inputs to the API are the center geo point and the radius of the circle in which you need to find items. The following is how the syntax of the query radius looks:

```
// center geo point
GeoPoint centerGeoPoint = new GeoPoint(18.514973, 73.850698);


// create query radius request
QueryRadiusRequest radiusRequest = new QueryRadiusRequest(
      centerGeoPoint, 200);
```

```
// invoke query result method
QueryRadiusResult radiusResult = geoDataManager
    .queryRadius(radiusRequest);

// Get items from the result
for (Map<String, AttributeValue> item : radiusResult.getItem()) {
  System.out.println("Item :" + item);
}
```

This would print all geo points that are in the 200-metre radius of the given center point. Internally, when we insert a geo point into DynamoDB, the geo hash gets calculated, and this geo hash is used to uniquely and exactly identify the location of geo points on planet Earth. This library also stores the geo hash as a separate attribute of an item. Hash stores the proximity of a nearby point, and for efficient retrieval it is stored as a local secondary index on items.

You can find examples of how to use this library on GitHub at `https://github.com/awslabs/dynamodb-geo/tree/master/samples`.

Language-specific libraries

There are various community-contributed libraries available for general use. In this section, I am going to list down all available libraries at present and some information about them.

Java

There are various libraries available in Java. They are explained in the following sections.

Jsoda

Jsoda provides simple Java object wrapping around the AWS API. You can simply create Java objects and annotate them correctly, and they are ready to use. This library provides similar interfaces for both SimpleDB and DynamoDB. Here POJOs are stored as records in DynamoDB. If you declare the attributes with primitive data types correctly, then the library automatically translates it into DynamoDB data types. This library also makes querying simple with features such as easy pagination options, caching, and so on.

You can get more information about the library at `https://github.com/williamw520/jsoda`.

Phoebe

This is another library that is a wrapper around the AWS API. This library simplifies the use of DynamoDB APIs. You can create a Phoebe object providing the user credentials and get started with the implementation. It also gives various data stores to be selected by users depending on their needs. A data store is simply a strategy of how you want to store your records and what kind of consistency you would like to choose.

This project is in its Alpha release, so use it with care. Currently, the project is hosted as a Google project at `https://code.google.com/p/phoebe-dynamodb/`.

Jcabi

This is yet another library that sits on top of AWS SDK APIs. It gives users a simplified interface to do CRUD operations on DynamoDB tables and items. To start using this library, you need to add a Maven dependency in `pom.xml` as follows:

```
<dependency>
  <groupId>com.jcabi</groupId>
  <artifactId>jcabi-dynamo</artifactId>
  <version>0.16</version>
</dependency>
```

This library is hosted on an independent website, where you can find more information about its usage at `http://dynamo.jcabi.com/`. We have already seen DynamoDB Local in *Chapter 1, Getting Started*, where we saw how to use DynamoDB Local for development purposes. Using this local version of DynamoDB, Jcabi has developed a Maven plugin that automatically starts DynamoDB Local to run unit tests. This is very helpful, as you can save money by not using actual DynamoDB and also continuously monitoring the tests suite in every build.

This project is hosted on GitHub at `https://github.com/jcabi/jcabi-dynamodb-maven-plugin`.

.NET

For those who are comfortable with the .NET framework, AWS has provided a complete SDK where you can perform DynamoDB operations in C#. In *Chapter 2, Data Models*, we have already seen some code snippets on how to use the .NET framework for DynamoDB operations.

You can learn more about it at `http://aws.amazon.com/sdkfornet/`.

Node.js

These days, along with primitive coding languages, Node.js is becoming popular in the coding community. So, if you are one of the Node.js users, then there are various libraries available that you can use directly to get started. Basically, these libraries give a DynamoDB client, which you can use to invoke various DynamoDB operations such as CRUDs.

Library Name	Description	Reference Link
dynode	Node.js client for DynamoDB	`https://github.com/Wantworthy/dynode`
awssum	DynamoDB operation supports	`https://github.com/awssum/awssum-amazon-dynamodb/`
dyndb	Relatively simple and smaller DynamoDB module	`https://github.com/serg-io/dyndb`
dynamite	This is a promise-based DynamoDB module implementation	`https://github.com/Medium/dynamite`
dynasaur	This is a Node.js-based ORM for DynamoDB	`http://tglines.github.io/dynasaur/`
Dynamo-client	A low-level DynamoDB client to access DynamoDB tables and items	`https://npmjs.org/package/dynamo-client`
Dynamo-table	Provides simple mapping between JS objects and DynamoDB tables	`https://www.npmjs.org/package/dynamo-table`
Dynasty	Provides simple and clean DynamoDB client.	`http://dynastyjs.com/`

Perl

For developers who code in Perl, there is a good number of libraries available, and some of them are as follows.

Net::Amazon::DynamoDB

The community has provided a DynamoDB interface using Perl. This a very simple library that provides access to DynamoDB tables/items using Perl. This does not support ORM-like modeling for DynamoDB.

You can find more information about it at `https://github.com/ukautz/Net-Amazon-DynamoDB`

Ruby

The following are some of the ready-to-use DynamoDB gems developed for Ruby developers.

Fog

Fog is a Ruby gem provided to interact with DynamoDB using Ruby. You can find more information about the library at `http://fog.io/`.

mince_dynamodb

This library provides ORM-like support and helps users map their objects to DynamoDB records. You can download the gem for this library at `http://rubygems.org/gems/mince_dynamo_db`.

dynamoid

This is again a Ruby gem that provides support for ORM-like mapping of objects with DynamoDB tables. It also supports easy querying and association support. The gem is available at `http://rubygems.org/gems/dynamoid`.

Others

There are libraries available in other languages also, which we didn't discuss earlier. The following is a table that gives reference to most such libraries:

Library Name	Language	Reference link
CFDynamo	Coldfusion	`http://www.craigkaminsky.me/2012/01/cfdynamo-cfc-wrapper-for-amazon.html`
Django-dynamodb-sessions	Django	`https://github.com/gtaylor/django-dynamodb-sessions`

Library Name	Language	Reference link
Dinerl	Erlang	`https://github.com/SemanticSugar/dinerl`
Ddb	Erlang	`https://github.com/wagerlabs/ddb`
Erlcloud	Erlang	`https://github.com/gleber/erlcloud/`
Goamz	Go	`https://github.com/crowdmob/goamz`
Groovy/Grails	DynamoDB GORM	`http://grails.org/plugin/dynamodb`

Tools

Like libraries, there are various tools available for general use. Some of the tools help to scale the DynamoDB database automatically, while some others help you do local testing of your code.

The following is a list of tools and their specifications.

Tools for testing

Considering the fact that each and every call to DynamoDB costs money, sometimes it gets difficult to use DynamoDB for the purposes of testing and development.

DynamoDB Local

We have already seen what DynamoDB local is in *Chapter 1, Getting Started*. Just to revisit, DynamoDB Local is a lightweight client-side database that roughly mimics the actual DynamoDB implementation. To enable DynamoDB Local, you need to download the JAR and run it using the next command. You can download the JAR at `http://dynamodb-local.s3-website-us-west-2.amazonaws.com/dynamodb_local_latest`. To run DynamoDB, you need to run the following command:

```
java -Djava.library.path=./DynamoDBLocal_lib -jar DynamoDBLocal.jar
```

There are various options available that you can explore. The information is available at `http://docs.aws.amazon.com/amazondynamodb/latest/developerguide/Tools.DynamoDBLocal.html`. The only prerequisite for this tool is that you should have Java/JDK installed on your machine.

Fake DynamoDB

Similar to what we have in DynamoDB Local, this Fake DynamoDB implementation emulates the actual DynamoDB functionality. Built in Ruby, it can be accessed and used by following some simple steps. To start the Fake DynamoDB service, you need to have Ruby 1.9+ installed. If you have it already, you can simply install the gem by running the following command:

```
gem install fake_dynamo --version 0.2.5
```

Once the gem is installed, you can start the service by running the following command:

```
fake_dynamo --port 4567
```

You can find some information about this tool at `https://github.com/ananthakumaran/fake_dynamo`.

The following tools are similar to the previously mentioned tools:

Tool	Reference Link
Alternator	`https://github.com/mboudreau/Alternator/`
Ddbmock	`https://pypi.python.org/pypi/ddbmock`
Client-side AWS	`https://github.com/perrystreetsoftware/clientside_aws`

Injecting failures

When working with services hosted by someone else, we have to rely on the service provider for everything. I am sure most of the users would surely be concerned about these things while using Amazon services. While designing any system, we always think about the failure scenarios as well, and we always consider such a case in our coding to avoid unexpected behavior of the system.

Today, what would happen to your application if DynamoDB starts giving delayed response or if it starts giving provisioned throughput exceeded exceptions and you are not prepared to handle a sudden burst? It's difficult to imagine, isn't it? So, to answer all such uncertainties, AWS has provided us with a framework called Request Handlers that allow you to inject latencies in response. It also allows you to test your code in the case of a provisioned throughput burst.

AWS SDK for Java contains a Request Handler, which can help you test your application for failures. You can simply inject the latencies, or you can throw a provisioned throughput and write code to see how your application can handle them if it happens actually.

You can find some more information about the usage and some sample implementation at the following links:

- `http://java.awsblog.com/post/Tx3I6AQJJXRW7EO/Injecting-Failures-and-Latency-using-the-AWS-SDK-for-Java`

- `https://github.com/awslabs/aws-dynamodb-examples/tree/master/inject-errors-latencies`

Tools for auto-scaling

We know that while creating a table in DynamoDB, we have to give information about the read and write capacity units. We also know that we can increase or decrease the value of read and write capacity units anytime depending on our need, but what if the demand bursts suddenly? And before you log in to the DynamoDB console and increase the provisioned throughput, we could lose some valuable requests coming from various clients. And losing any such data may cost a lot for any enterprise. So how do we solve this problem? Is there any tool available that would automatically increase the demand before the burst and reduce the demand whenever there are not many requests coming in? The answer is, yes! Now, let's discuss one such tool.

Dynamic DynamoDB

We have a community-contributed tool that automatically scales the DynamoDB provisioned throughput, and the name of that tool is Dynamic DynamoDB. This tool includes the following features:

- This tool automatically scales the tables up and down.

- There is a provision to restrict auto-scaling for a certain time slot.

- It's easy to use and integrate with your application.

- There is a provision to set maximum and minimum read and write capacity.

- This tool provides the functionality of monitoring multiple DynamoDB tables at a time.

- This tool gives you notifications on scale up or scale down of provisioned throughput.
- This tool checks if the application is up and running before doing any scale up/down activities. This can be helpful if your application is facing some other issues, because of which the requests are low.

There are various ways of using Dynamic DynamoDB. One of them is to use a CloudFormation template that launches a `t1.micro` EC2 instance with preconfigured Dynamic DynamoDB. Another way is to install the tool by cloning it from Git repo.

The CloudFormation template is available at `http://raw.github.com/sebdah/dynamic-dynamodb/master/cloudformation-templates/dynamic-dynamodb.json`.

To install Dynamic DynamoDB manually you can refer to `http://dynamic-dynamodb.readthedocs.org/en/latest/installation.html`.

Dynamic DynamoDB is a service that you can start, stop, and restart easily. So, whenever you need this service, you can use it just by starting with a command. When we configure this tool, we need to provide user credentials. This user needs full access to the DynamoDB tables so that modifications can be done easily. You can also create a dedicated user with the following accesses:

- cloudwatch:GetMetricStatistics
- dynamodb:DescribeTable
- dynamodb:ListTables
- dynamodb:UpdateTable
- sns:Publish (to send in notifications)

To know more about the tool, please visit the `http://dynamic-dynamodb.readthedocs.org/en/latest/index.html` URL.

Tools for backup and archival

Archiving data from any database is always one of the biggest needs. We have already seen how to archive data on AWS S3 using EMR, but there is one simple community-contributed tool, written in Node.js that helps archive data on S3. This tool saves DynamoDB data in JSON format. It also gives you the functionality to restore the archived data to DynamoDB. Let's discuss this tool in detail.

DynamoDB Table Archiver

DynamoDB Table Archiver consists of two simple Node.js scripts that fetch the data from source tables and save it on S3. To use these scripts, you need to have Node. js installed. The source code of the tool is available on GitHub at `https://github. com/yegor256/dynamo-archive`.

Summary

In this chapter, we started with exploring AWS-provided Java libraries, that is, the Transaction library and the Geo library. The Transaction library enabled multi-item atomic operations, where we can simply use the API and perform the operations without any doubts about inconsistent states. Geo library enabled us to easily save geographical points and query them with simple APIs, such as Query radius and Query rectangle.

We also listed down well-known language-specific libraries to enable developers to manipulate DynamoDB data with a language of their own choice. Similarly, we also explored some tools that would help us in testing DynamoDB locally, auto-scaling the tables, and archiving data on AWS S3.

In our next chapter, we are going to see how DynamoDB can be used to back mobile applications and how it will help your mobile applications to scale easily.

9
Developing Mobile Apps Using DynamoDB

Today, one of the coolest things every developer wants to do is to create their own mobile application, launch it for public access, have it go viral, and then have some big technology firm buy it for billions of dollars, isn't it? Of course! Why not? Today we see that mobile devices are more popular than regular desktops. It would not be an exaggeration if I say, in a decade or so, most of the nonmobile devices would vanish away.

Keeping this in mind, mobile applications are very important in all perspectives. In this chapter, we will see:

- Why you should choose DynamoDB as a backend to your mobile application
- What options to implement authentication and authorization it gives
- How you should perform various operations using the AWS SDK for Android and iOS

Many of you might have already developed an Android or iOS application, for which you would have been using some web server where your application and database would be accessed from. Having a scalable, easily accessible database is one of the biggest needs. There are many problems and challenges in going ahead with traditional web hosting services, which are mentioned as follows:

- Purchasing a host/device from the service providers
- Selecting and installing a database from a variety of databases
- Maintaining the database

- If the database is not scalable, then migration of the application to some other database

- Initial investment is required to purchase the host

- As the pay-per model is not in use, you need to pay for the complete service duration (minimum 1 year for most of the web hosting service providers) even if the application does not do well in the market

So what could be done in this case? Is there any better way to store mobile application data? The answer is yes. Amazon provides SDKs for iOS and Android operating systems where you can simply use the given APIs to manipulate the data. Here are some advantages of using DynamoDB as your database for your mobile application:

- It is easy to use and configure.

- It provides support for Web Identity Federation (can use user identity from websites such as Facebook, Google, and Amazon).

- It has a scalable architecture; you can set the read and write capacity units as per the need. If the application goes viral, you can simply increase the capacity units or reduce the capacity units when the load is low.

- It is a pay-per-use model and, hence, cost effective.

- It is easy to integrate with other AWS devices if required.

- It has a faster response time compared to other RDBMS databases, which is very much required for a mobile application.

- There is no need to implement a separate proxy server to generate authentication tokens.

Authentication and Authorization

I am sure that by now, you would have started thinking about developing an app using DynamoDB as the backend database. But wait! There is one small problem with it, that is, mobile application codes always need to be deployed on each app user's mobile. This means that if we need to access AWS resources, we would also need to send in the security credentials with each app, which is not a good thing to do from the security point of view. Encrypting the credentials would help in reducing the risk, but it would not completely make the app secure as by putting in some effort, hackers would also get hold of the encrypted credentials.

Also, considering that eventually the app would have a huge number of users, we cannot create separate user accounts in IAM. So, even this would not help us. So what can be done in this case? For that we have two options:

- Use web identity federation
- Create your own custom authentication

Let's try to understand the process in detail.

Using Web Identity Federation

We have already seen what Web Identity Federation is in *Chapter 5*, *Advanced Topics*. Just to revise, WIF is a utility that allows end users to access an AWS resource using accounts such as Amazon, Facebook, and Google. Here, we use **Secure Token Service** (**STS**) from Amazon to generate temporary user credentials, and by using those credentials, we access the AWS resource (for example, a table in DynamoDB). The following steps will help you to implement WIF for your application:

1. Register your application with identity providers such as Amazon, Google, and Facebook. These identity providers have given elaborate description on how to register your app. You can follow the steps to validate the identity of the user.

2. Once you have got the identity token from the providers, you can call the `AssumeRoleWithWebIdentity` API, which is a part of AWS STS, to get the temporary credentials. To call `AsssumeRoleWithWebIdentity`, you don't need any credentials. Once you call this API with the required details, you would get temporary credentials, that is, access key and secret key. You can read more about this API at `http://docs.aws.amazon.com/STS/latest/APIReference/API_AssumeRoleWithWebIdentity.html`.

3. Using these credentials, you can call AWS APIs (for example, an API to put data in a DynamoDB table API to read something from the DynamoDB table). These credentials would be valid for only a given time. This time could be from 15 minutes to 1 hour. Depending on your need, you can set the validity duration.

4. Once the credentials get timed out, you need to again pass on the identity token to STS and get new, temporary credentials.

This is explained in the following diagram:

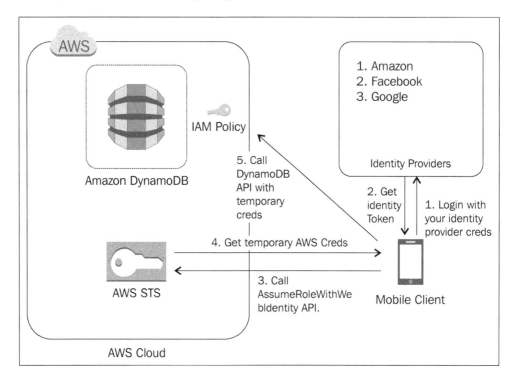

To understand WIF in a better way, you can check out the following link where you can actually see how WIF works live:

```
https://web-identity-federation-playground.s3.amazonaws.com/index.html
```

Creating your own custom authentication

Some people might not want to integrate their application with other companies, such as Facebook, Google, or Amazon, as it creates a dependency on them, and if some day, any one of these companies stops giving identity tokens, then as an app developer or owner, you would be in big trouble. So, is there any way other than shipping actual AWS credentials with your app code? The answer is yes!

In this case, you need to implement your own identity store, and you need to give the identity token. You can use AWS EC2 or your own server to deploy your identity store and direct all your requests to this store to get the secure token. And the rest remains the same. I mean that once you have an identity token from your own provider, you can then call STS to get temporary credentials, and once you have the credentials, you can access the DynamoDB API to perform the operation. This is demonstrated in the following diagram:

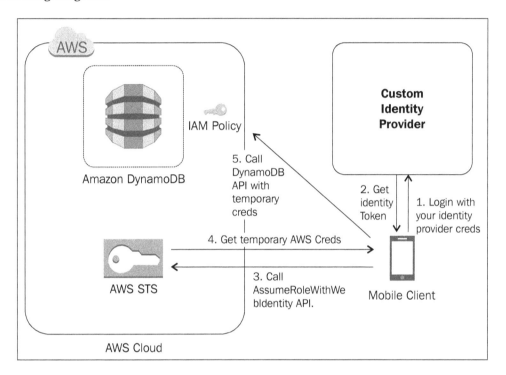

Performing operations using mobile SDKs

Amazon has given an SDK to leading mobile platforms, such as iOS and Android. We can make use of it to perform operations in a mobile application. With these simplified SDK APIs, it is very easy to do normal database operations on DynamoDB. You just need to create a design database schema, and invoke various requests to add/delete and update database entries.

With the ease of integration with other AWS services, using DynamoDB for your mobile application gives you a great advantage. You can download the SDKs from the following URLs:

- **For Android**: `http://sdk-for-android.amazonwebservices.com/latest/aws-android-sdk.zip`

- **For iOS**: `http://sdk-for-ios.amazonwebservices.com/latest/aws-ios-sdk.zip`

To get started, you can download sample Android applications from GitHub from the following URL:

`https://github.com/awslabs/aws-sdk-android-samples`

Now, let's get started with understanding operations for the iOS and Android platforms.

Writing data to DynamoDB

We have already seen how to create, delete, and update using various APIs in *Chapter 2*, *Data Models*. In this section, we will go through the APIs available for the iOS and Android SDKs. To understand this in a better way, let's assume that you want to develop an app where a user can post adds to sell, rent, or purchase anything. For that, we would need a table called product table, which would look like this:

productId	recordId	Data
123	productName	BMW Z
123	cost	$20000
456	productName	Hill range bicycle
456	cost	$120
789	productName	Baseball bat
789	Cost	$50

Here, we would like to have the hash key as `productId` and the range key as `recordId`.

Android

Now, let's see how to write code in **Android** to add items in the `Product` table:

```
// Hash Map for storing attributes
Map<String,AttributeValue> product = new HashMap<String,
AttributeValue>();


// Adding hash key and value
item.put("productId", new AttributeValue().withS("123"));


// Adding range key and value
item.put("recordId", new AttributeValue().withS("productName"));

// Adding actual data for corresponding key
item.put("data", new AttributeValue().withSS("BMW Z"));

// Invoke put item request with proper table name
PutItemRequest putItemRequest = new PutItemRequest("ProductTable",
  item);

// process the request
PutItemResult putItemResult =
  dynamoClient.putItem(putItemRequest);
```

We have already seen multiple times how to create a DynamoDB client and configure it with your own AWS credentials.

iOS

To perform the same operation on an iOS platform, you need to write something like this:

```
// create put item request
DynamoDBPutItemRequest *putItemRequest = [DynamoDBPutItemRequest new];

// Set table name
request.tableName = @"ProductTable";

// create DynamoDBAttributeValue for hash key
```

```
DynamoDBAttributeValue *value = [[DynamoDBAttributeValue alloc]
  initWithS:@"123"];
[request.item setValue:value forKey:@"productId"];

//create and set range key
value = [[DynamoDBAttributeValue alloc] initWithS:@"ProductName"];
[request.item setValue:value forKey:@"recordId"];

// Add actual data corresponding to keys

value = [DynamoDBAttributeValue new];
[value addS:@"BMW Z"];
[request.item setValue:value forKey:@"data"];

// process the request
DynamoDBPutItemResponse *response = [self.dynamoClient
  putItem:request];
```

Getting consumed capacity information

There are options available to get information about the consumed capacity units for each DynamoDB call. These options would help you monitor the throughput you are consuming for each request. By getting this information, we can see which operation is consuming more read and write units, and then we can tune it to use minimal resources.

We can also use this information to measure the throughput for a certain number of requests. This would help us manage our resources in a better way. Let's go through the syntax to get the read and write capacity units.

Android

Here is a code snippet to get the consumed capacity units for DynamoDB calls:

```
// Set the type of capacity units you need to get info about. Here we
want both //read and write so setting it to be TOTAL

putItemRequest.setReturnConsumedCapacity(ReturnConsumedCapacity.
TOTAL);

// Invoke the request
PuttItemResult result = ddbClient.putItem(putItemRequest);

// Log our consumed capacity
Log.i(LOG_TAG, "Consumed write capacity for putItem: = " +
  result.getConsumedCapacity().getCapacityUnits().intValue());
```

iOS

Here is a code snippet to get the consumed capacity units for DynamoDB calls:

```
// Set the type of capacity units you need to get info about. Here we
want both //read and write so setting it to be TOTAL
putItemRequest.returnConsumedCapacity = @"TOTAL";

// Invoke the request
DynamoDBPutItemResponse *putItemResponse = [self.ddb
  putItem:putItemRequest];

// Log our consumed capacity
NSLog(@"Consumed write capacity for putItem: %d",
  [putItemResponse.consumedCapacity.capacityUnits integerValue]);
```

Conditional writes

We know that the putItem request first searches for the records with given keys; if it finds any matching record, then it replaces the record with a new value. If it does not find any matching record, it simply inserts it as a new record. This can be dangerous and may lead to unwanted record update. So to avoid this, you can perform conditional writes on items, in which you pass on a flag that first checks whether the value is already present; if yes, then do not add anything, and if not present, then only add a new value.

Android

Here is how we use conditional writes using the AWS SDK for Android:

```
// Create map for expected attribute value
Map<String,ExpectedAttributeValue> expectedAttri = new HashMap<String,
ExpectedAttributeValue>();

//set attribute whose value you need to check
expectedAttri.put("recordId", new ExpectedAttributeValue().
withExists(false));

// set the same in request
putItemRequest.setExpected(expectedAttri);
```

We can also use `ExpectedAttributeValue` to implement a counter. An atomic counter means that you want the value to be updated correctly and to always reflect the exact value. For example, in our `Product` table, if we have an attribute, say, number of items in stock, this attribute always needs to be in the exact state, so we can create an atomic counter using `ExpectedAttributeValue` as shown in the following code:

```
// Create a request which updates the no. of items in stock
Map<String,AttributeValue> item = new HashMap<String,
AttributeValue>();
item.put("productId", new AttributeValue().withN("777"));
item.put("recordId", new
  AttributeValue().withS("NoOfItemsInStock"));
item.put("data", new AttributeValue().withS("3"));

PutItemRequest putItemRequest = new PutItemRequest("ProductTable",
item);

// Here we want DynamoDB to update the record only when its value is 2
AttributeValue itemCounter = new AttributeValue().withS("2");

Map<String,ExpectedAttributeValue> expected = new
  HashMap<String,ExpectedAttributeValue>();
expected.put("data", new
  ExpectedAttributeValue().withValue(itemCounter));

putItemRequest.setExpected(expected);

//Invoke the request
PutItemResult putItemResult = ddbClient.putItem(putItemRequest);
```

If the value present in a DynamoDB table does not match with the expected value, it throws `ConditionalCheckFailedException`; it is always a good practice to catch an exception, try to fetch the current value in DynamoDB, and then retry the request as shown in the following code:

```
try {

  // Invoke request

  PutItemResult putItemResult = ddbClient.putItem(putItemRequest);
}

catch (ConditionalCheckFailedException error) {
```

```
    // Conditional write failed because of unexpected value in
DynamoDB
    // Fetch the current value and retry the request

}
```

iOS

The syntax for conditional writes in iOS is as follows:

 The next piece of code checks whether any item with given details exists; if not, then only the code commits the put request.

```
DynamoDBExpectedAttributeValue *checkExists =
    [DynamoDBExpectedAttributeValue new];
checkExists.exists = NO;
[putItemRequest.expected setValue:checkExists forKey:@"recordId"];
```

 The next piece of code checks if the value of data is two, only then does it update it to a new value three.

```
// Create a request which updates the no. of items in stock
DynamoDBPutItemRequest *putItemRequest = [DynamoDBPutItemRequest
    new];
request.tableName = @"ProductTable";

DynamoDBAttributeValue *value = [[DynamoDBAttributeValue alloc]
    initWithN:@"777"]; [putItemRequest.item setValue:value
    forKey:@"productId"];
value = [[DynamoDBAttributeValue alloc]
    initWithS:@"NoOfItemsInStock"];

[putItemRequest.item setValue:value forKey:@"recordId"];
value = [[DynamoDBAttributeValue alloc] initWithS:@"3"];

[putItemRequest.item setValue:value forKey:@"data"];


// Here we want DynamoDB to update the record only when its value is 2

value = [[DynamoDBAttributeValue alloc] initWithS:@"2"];
```

```
DynamoDBExpectedAttributeValue *attr =
  [[DynamoDBExpectedAttributeValue alloc] initWithValue:value];

// Set the expected value in put item request
[putItemRequest.expected setValue:checkExists forKey:@"data"];

// invoke the request
DynamoDBPutItemResponse *putItemResponse = [self.ddb
putItem:putItemRequest];
```

If the client finds an unexpected value for the given attribute, then it fails the request with an error. Hence, it is recommended to check for an erroneous code so that we can handle the failure by retrying the request as shown in the following code:

```
// Invoke request
DynamoDBPutItemResponse *putItemResponse = [self.ddb
  putItem:putItemRequest];

if(nil != putItemReponse.error) {
  NSString *errorCode = [response.error.userInfo
    objectForKey:@"errorCode"];

    if ([errorCode isEqualToString:@"ConditionalCheckFailedExcepti
on"]) {
  // Conditional write failed because of unexpected value in DynamoDB
  // Fetch the current value and retry the request
      ...
  }
  else {
      // some other error occurred
      ...
  }
```

 Earlier, AWS SDKs used to throw exceptions if any issue came up with the invoked request. This forced developers to surround any code written for AWS with try/catch blocks, which was a nasty thing. So, in order to avoid this, AWS started providing error codes with NSError or NSException. So, with this approach, if any error occurs, the AWS SDK sets it in an error property. Hence, it is recommended to check an error property to nil before continuing with the next code. If required, we can also enable the exception back.

You can read more about exception handling in iOS at http://mobile.awsblog. com/post/Tx2PZV371MJJHUG/How-Not-to-Throw-Exceptions-with-the-AWS- SDK-for-iOS

Deleting an item

To delete an item, we need to provide the key details for the given item in the delete item request and invoke the same request as follows.

Android

Here is a code sample that explains how to delete an item from a DynamoDB table:

```
// create a map, specifying the key attributes of the item to be
deleted
Map<String,AttributeValue> key = new HashMap<String,AttributeValue>();

key.put("productId", new AttributeValue().withN("123"));

key.put("recordId", new AttributeValue().withS("productName"));

// create  delete item request

DeleteItemRequest deleteItemRequest = new DeleteItemRequest("ProductT
able", key);

// invoke the request

DeleteItemResult deleteItemResponse =
  ddbClient.deleteItem(deleteItemRequest);
```

iOS

Here is a syntax to delete an item from a DynamoDB table using an iOS SDK:

```
// create  delete item request

DynamoDBDeleteItemRequest *deleteItemRequest =
  [DynamoDBDeleteItemRequest new];
request.tableName = @"ProductTable";

// Specifying the key attributes of the item to be deleted

DynamoDBAttributeValue *value = [[DynamoDBAttributeValue alloc]
  initWithN:@"123"];

[deleteItemRequest.key setValue:value forKey:@"productId"];
value = [[DynamoDBAttributeValue alloc] initWithS:@"productName"];
```

```
[deleteItemRequest.key setValue:value forKey:@"recordId"];

// Invoke the request
DynamoDBDeleteItemResponse *deleteItemResponse = [self.ddb
  deleteItem:deleteItemRequest];
```

Fetching data

Earlier, we saw how to put data into DynamoDB tables. Now, let's see how to fetch the stored data back using mobile SDK APIs.

Android

Here is the syntax to fetch the data from a given DynamoDB table:

```
//specify the key attributes for the record to be fetched
Map<String, AttributeValue> key = new HashMap<String,
AttributeValue>();
key.put("productId", 123);
key.put("recordId", "productName");

// Create request
GetItemRequest getItemRequest = new GetItemRequest("ProductTable",k
ey);

// Invoke request
GetItemResult getItemResult = ddbClient.getItem(getItemRequest);
```

Once you have the result, you can fetch the required attribute from an item.

iOS

Here is the syntax to fetch the data from a given DynamoDB table:

```
// Create request and specify the table name
DynamoDBGetItemRequest *getItemRequest = [DynamoDBGetItemRequest new];
getItemRequest.tableName = @"ProductTable";

// Specify the keys for the item to be fetched.
DynamoDBAttributeValue *productId = [[DynamoDBAttributeValue alloc]
initWithN:@"123"];

DynamoDBAttributeValue *recordId = [[DynamoDBAttributeValue alloc]
initWithS:@"productName"];
```

```
getItemRequest.key = [NSMutableDictionary dictionaryWithObjectsAndKeys
:productId, @"productId", recordId, @"recordId", nil];

DynamoDBGetItemResponse *getItemResponse = [self.ddb
getItem:getItemRequest];

// the value of the attribute you wish to fetch from the results
DynamoDBAttributeValue  *productNameValue = [getItemResponse.item
valueForKey:@"data"];
```

Querying data

For the product table use case, sometimes there might be a need to get all details for the given product ID; in that case you use query API to fetch the details. All other limitations of query APIs, which we discussed in *Chapter 2*, *Data Models*, applies here as well; for example, in a single client call, we can fetch data only up to 1 MB. If the query result size is more than 1 MB, then pagination is provided. We can use `lastEvaluatedKey` to fetch the next set of results.

The following code snippets show how to fetch all the data for a given product ID using queries with the Android and iOS SDKs.

Android

Here is the syntax to fetch the data from a given DynamoDB table using query API:

```
// specify the query condition, here product id = 123
Condition hashKeyCondition = new Condition()
    .withComparisonOperator(ComparisonOperator.EQ.toString())
    .withAttributeValueList(new AttributeValue().withN("123"));

Map<String, Condition> keyConditions = new HashMap<String,
Condition>();
keyConditions.put("productId", hashKeyCondition);


Map<String, AttributeValue> lastEvaluatedKey = null;
do {

    QueryRequest queryRequest = new QueryRequest()
      .withTableName("ProductTable")
      .withKeyConditions(keyConditions)
      .withExclusiveStartKey(lastEvaluatedKey);
```

```
QueryResult queryResult = dynamoDBClient.query(queryRequest);

    // Get all items from query result
    queryResult.getItems();

// If the response lastEvaluatedKey has contents, that means there are
more    // results
    lastEvaluatedKey = queryResult.getLastEvaluatedKey();
} while (lastEvaluatedKey != null);
```

iOS

Here is the syntax to fetch data from a given DynamoDB table using a query API:

```
// specify the query condition, here product id = 123

DynamoDBCondition *condition = [DynamoDBCondition new];
condition.comparisonOperator = @"EQ";

DynamoDBAttributeValue *productId = [[DynamoDBAttributeValue
  alloc] initWithN:@"123"];

[condition addAttributeValueList:productId];

NSMutableDictionary *queryStartKey = nil;
do {

    DynamoDBQueryRequest *queryRequest = [DynamoDBQueryRequest
      new];
    queryRequest.tableName = @"ProductTable";
    queryRequest.exclusiveStartKey = queryStartKey;

    queryRequest.keyConditions = [NSMutableDictionary
      dictionaryWithObject:condition forKey:@"productId"];

    DynamoDBQueryResponse *queryResponse = [[Constants ddb]
      query:queryRequest];

    // Each item in the result set is a NSDictionary of
DynamoDBAttributeValue
    for (NSDictionary *item in queryResponse.items) {
      DynamoDBAttributeValue *recordId = [item
        objectForKey:@"recordId"];
        NSLog(@"record id = '%@'", recordId.s);
    }
```

```
// If the response lastEvaluatedKey has contents, that means there are
more      // results
    queryStartKey = queryResponse.lastEvaluatedKey;

} while ([queryStartKey count] != 0
```

Consistent reads

As we know, DynamoDB is eventually consistent and gives option to users to set the type of reads they wish to see. Sometimes, application operations cannot tolerate an eventually consistent model. In that case, you can explicitly set consistency to 'strongly consistent'.

Here are the code snippets which show you how to set the consistency for a given request.

Android

Consistency in reads can be set for `GetItem` and query APIs as follows:

```
// GetItem set strong consistent reads
GetItemRequest getItemRequest = new GetItemRequest("ProductTable",key)
    .withConsistentRead(true);

// Configure and invoke the request
..

// Query set strong consistent reads
QueryRequest queryRequest = new QueryRequest()
    .withTableName("ProductTable")
    .withConsistentRead(true);

// Configure and invoke the request
..
iOS
Here is how we set the strongly consistent reads for the get item and
query APIs in iOS SDK.
// GetItem with consistent reads
DynamoDBGetItemRequest *getItemRequest = [DynamoDBGetItemRequest new];
getItemRequest.tableName = @"ProductTable";

getItemRequest.consistentRead = YES;
```

```
// Configure and invoke the request
..


// Query with consistent reads
DynamoDBQueryRequest *queryRequest = [DynamoDBQueryRequest new];
queryRequest.tableName = @"ProductTable";


queryRequest.consistentRead = YES;


// Configure and invoke the request
```

Using local secondary indexes

We have already seen the local secondary indexes in *Chapter 2, Data Models*. So, if someone wants to query a DynamoDB table data using attributes other than the primary key attributes, then we need to use local secondary index.

Suppose we modify our product table to accommodate one more attribute named `lastModifiedBy`, this attribute would be updated every time some user makes changes to it. Our requirement is to find the change made by a certain user for a given product ID. To do so, we need to create a local secondary index on `lastModifiedBy`. Here is how the table will look now:

productId (hash key)	recordId (range key)	Data	lastModifiedBy (Local Secondary Index)
123	`productName`	BMW Z	Alice
123	cost	$20000	Bob
456	`productName`	Hill range bicycle	Alice
456	cost	$120	Alice
789	`productName`	Base ball bat	Bob
789	cost	$50	Bob

Android

Here is how we have to write queries to fetch an attribute modified by a certain user:

```
// create map for keys
Map keyConditions = new HashMap();

// Specify the key conditions , here product id = 123
Condition hashKeyCondition = new Condition()
    .withComparisonOperator(ComparisonOperator.EQ.toString())
    .withAttributeValueList(new AttributeValue().withN("123"));
keyConditions.put("productId", hashKeyCondition);

// Specify condition for index, here lastModifiedBy == Alice
 Condition lastModCondition = new Condition()
    .withComparisonOperator(ComparisonOperator.EQ.toString())
    .withAttributeValueList(new AttributeValue().withS("Alice"));
keyConditions.put("lastModifiedBy", lastModCondition);

Map lastEvaluatedKey = null;
do {
    QueryRequest queryRequest = new QueryRequest()
            .withTableName("ProductTable")
            .withKeyConditions(keyConditions)
            .withExclusiveStartKey(lastEvaluatedKey)
            .withIndexName("lastModifiedBy-index");

    QueryResult queryResult = client.query(queryRequest);
    // Use query results
..
    // check if there are more records for the query
    lastEvaluatedKey = queryResult.getLastEvaluatedKey();
} while (lastEvaluatedKey != null)
```

iOS

Here is how we have to write queries to fetch an attribute modified by a certain user.

```
// Create our dictionary of conditions
NSDictionary *conditions = [NSMutableDictionary new];

// Specify the key conditions , here product id = 123
DynamoDBCondition *productIdCondition = [DynamoDBCondition new];
```

```
condition.comparisonOperator = @"EQ";
DynamoDBAttributeValue *productId = [[DynamoDBAttributeValue alloc]
initWithN:@"123"];

[productIdCondition addAttributeValueList:productId];
[conditions setObject: productIdCondition forKey:@"productId"];

// Specify the key conditions , here product id = 123
DynamoDBCondition *lastModifiedCondition = [DynamoDBCondition new];
lastModifiedCondition.comparisonOperator = @"EQ";
DynamoDBAttributeValue *userName = [[DynamoDBAttributeValue alloc]
initWithS:@"Alice"];
[lastModifiedCondition addAttributeValueList:userName];
[conditions setObject:lastModifiedCondition forKey:@"lastModifiedBy"];

NSMutableDictionary *queryStartKey = nil;
do {
    DynamoDBQueryRequest *queryRequest = [DynamoDBQueryRequest new];
    queryRequest.tableName = @"ProductTable";
    queryRequest.exclusiveStartKey = queryStartKey;

    // specify the local secondary index
    queryRequest.keyConditions = conditions;
    queryRequest.indexName = @"lastModifiedBy-index";

    // Invoke query
    DynamoDBQueryResponse *queryResponse = [[Constants ddb]
query:queryRequest];

    // Use query results
    ..

    // check if there are more records for the query
    queryStartKey = queryResponse.lastEvaluatedKey;

} while ([queryStartKey count] != 0);
```

Summary

In this chapter, we discussed considering AWS DynamoDB as a backend database for your mobile applications. We started with discussing the challenges in using traditional in-house databases for mobile applications. We then discussed how DynamoDB can be helpful if you chose it as a backend database for mobile applications.

We talked about how WIF can help you to reduce the time to market for mobile applications by integrating the authentication and authorization with Facebook, Google, and Amazon accounts. We also saw how the AWS STS helps in securing our mobile applications by generating temporary access tokens for mobile application requests on AWS resources. For those who want to use their own identity credentials, we saw how that can be performed as well.

Later, we discussed the best practices in DynamoDB data modeling for a mobile considering an example use case of an e-commerce mobile application. Taking this example as a reference, we understood how various operations can be performed using AWS Mobile SDKs for Android and iOS.

I hope this helps you, providing proper direction for your understanding and development.

At last, now that we have gone through most of the features, pros and cons, usages, code samples and designs of DynamoDB, I hope this book contributes to your knowledge. All the best for your adventures with DynamoDB!

Index

C

D

time series data
  managing 95
tools
  for auto-scaling 179
  for backup/archival 180
  for testing 177
  using 177
Transaction library
  about 165, 166
  atomic writes 166-168
  isolated reads 169
  URL 169
try block 126

U

uncommitted reads 169
updateItem method 50, 58
UpdateItem operation 12
UpdateTable operation 11
use cases, DynamoDB
  bookstore application 153
  knowledge market website 153, 158

V

vector clocks 80

W

web hosting services
  challenges 183, 184
web identity federation
  about 122, 123
  implementing 185, 186
  URL 186
www.StackOverflow.com 158

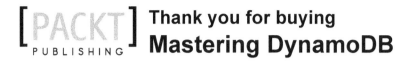

Thank you for buying
Mastering DynamoDB

About Packt Publishing

Packt, pronounced 'packed', published its first book "*Mastering phpMyAdmin for Effective MySQL Management*" in April 2004 and subsequently continued to specialize in publishing highly focused books on specific technologies and solutions.

Our books and publications share the experiences of your fellow IT professionals in adapting and customizing today's systems, applications, and frameworks. Our solution based books give you the knowledge and power to customize the software and technologies you're using to get the job done. Packt books are more specific and less general than the IT books you have seen in the past. Our unique business model allows us to bring you more focused information, giving you more of what you need to know, and less of what you don't.

Packt is a modern, yet unique publishing company, which focuses on producing quality, cutting-edge books for communities of developers, administrators, and newbies alike. For more information, please visit our website: www.packtpub.com.

Writing for Packt

We welcome all inquiries from people who are interested in authoring. Book proposals should be sent to author@packtpub.com. If your book idea is still at an early stage and you would like to discuss it first before writing a formal book proposal, contact us; one of our commissioning editors will get in touch with you.

We're not just looking for published authors; if you have strong technical skills but no writing experience, our experienced editors can help you develop a writing career, or simply get some additional reward for your expertise.

Talend for Big Data

ISBN: 978-1-78216-949-9   Paperback: 96 pages

Access, transform, and integrate data using Talend's open source, extensible tools

1. Write complex processing job codes easily with the help of clear and step-by-step instructions.

2. Compare, filter, evaluate, and group vast quantities of data using Hadoop Pig.

3. Explore and perform HDFS and RDBMS integration with the Sqoop component.

Big Data Analytics with R and Hadoop

ISBN: 978-1-78216-328-2   Paperback: 238 pages

Set up an integrated infrastructure of R and Hadoop to turn your data analytics into Big Data analytics

1. Write Hadoop MapReduce within R.

2. Learn data analytics with R and the Hadoop platform.

3. Handle HDFS data within R.

4. Understand Hadoop streaming with R.

Please check **www.PacktPub.com** for information on our titles

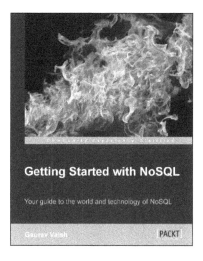

Getting Started with NoSQL

ISBN: 978-1-84969-498-8   Paperback: 142 pages

Your guide to the world and technology of NoSQL

1. First hand, detailed information about NoSQL technology.

2. Learn the differences between NoSQL and RDBMS and where each is useful.

3. Understand the various data models for NoSQL.

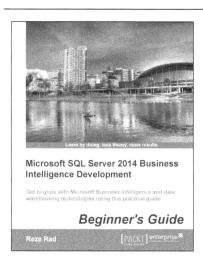

Microsoft SQL Server 2014 Business Intelligence Development Beginner's Guide

ISBN: 978-1-84968-888-8   Paperback: 350 pages

Get to grips with Microsoft Business Intelligence and data warehousing technologies using this practical guide

1. Discover the Dimensional Modeling concept while designing a data warehouse.

2. Learn Data Movement based on technologies such as SSIS, MDS, and DQS.

3. Design dashboards and reports with Microsoft BI technologies.

Please check **www.PacktPub.com** for information on our titles

www.ingramcontent.com/pod-product-compliance
Lightning Source LLC
Chambersburg PA
CBHW060548060326
40690CB00017B/3640